水からの伝言

世界初!! 水の 氷結 結晶写真集

The Message from Water

The Message from Water is telling us to take a look at ourselves.

The Message from Water is telling us to take a look at ourselves.

The Message from Water is telling us to take a look at ourselves.

江本 勝（国際波動友の会 会長 / IHM総合研究所 所長）／IHM総合研究所

波動教育社

Index
Contents

じめに

国際波動友の会　会長　江本勝
Masaru Emoto, Chairman of International HADO Membership

江本勝と水と波動と

　私と水との出会いは、リー・H・ロレンツェン博士との出会いにはじまります。リー博士が34歳、私が41歳の頃のことでした。リー博士はカリフォルニアのバークレイ校でバイオケミカル・生物化学を学び、その後、水の研究者となり『マイクロクラスター水（共鳴磁場水）』（121ページ参照）を開発した人です。

　リー博士に出会って水に魅せられた男が、それをもっと知りたいと思ったことから拡がり、水を測る、水を見る機械はないだろうか……と探しました。するとまたリー博士の紹介でMRA『＝Magnetic Resonance Analyzer（共鳴磁場分析器）』という波動を測定する機械に出会い、私の水から波動への研究が加速度的に進んでいきました。

　MRAという波動測定機は、アメリカではホメオパシー（ドイツで盛んな薬療法）のために使われていました。私はこの機械に出会った瞬間に、『マイクロクラスター水（共鳴磁場水）』と結びつけてみたらどうか……と、ひらめくものがあり、これを日本に持ち帰り、研究をすすめました。

　その結果、私がリー博士に依頼してつくってもらったマイクロクラスター水に、MRAによる波動情報を転写した『波動水』は、水に含まれる情報の違いから、水によって体調が改善されることが実証されました。その技術をもって健康相談をしながら、なおも水を追及し続けました。

　MRAと波動ついては、次にあげる私の著作において、すでに発表されておりますので、もっと詳しくお知りになりたい方は、ご参照ください。

『波動時代への序幕』サンロード出版
『波動の人間学』ビジネス社
『波動の真理』ＰＨＰ研究所
『波動と水と生命と』ＰＨＰ研究所
『波動の食品学』菅原明子氏と共著　高輪出版社
『宇宙意識と波動』
　　　ラビ・バトラ氏と共著　ＰＨＰ研究所
『波動革命』ＰＨＰ研究所
『波動の幸福論』ＰＨＰ研究所
『波動学のすすめ』ＰＨＰ研究所
『波動とは何か』ＰＨＰ研究所
『甦る潜在記憶』ＰＨＰ研究所

　本著では、水の研究をするうちに、いろいろな水を氷結させて結晶写真を撮影するようになり、水の顔を見た……という経験から、「水からの伝言」を写真集というかたちでお伝えしたいと思います。

水と人間と地球と

　人間が物質的にはじめてこの地球上にその姿を現わすとき、それは母親の卵子と父親の精子が巡り会って受精し、受精卵となったときです。このとき水の占める割合は95％。つまり、ほとんど水ということです。そして、成人した人間の身体のなかの水分量は70％。だから人間は水からできていると言ってもいいくらいなのです。そして人は死ぬまで、毎日いろいろな「水」に囲まれて暮らしています。

　地球は「水の惑星」と呼ばれ、表面の約70％は水でおお

われています。なんだか人間とよく似ていますね。

そして、その水の大部分は「海」にあり、雲や霧になって空気中を漂っている「水」もあれば、雨水、地下水、湖や沼、河川、高い山の万年雪、南極などの「氷」も、もともとは「水」です。

でも大切な水が、良い水なのか、悪い水なのか、人間の身体にとってはどうかとなると、研究機関か専門家でない限り、はっきりしたことはわかりません。私たちからみれば、どの水も同じようにみえますから。

水に含まれる情報の違いとはなんだろうか。なんとかそれを見ることはできないだろうか。

そんなとき、ふと、『まだ科学が解けない疑問』（ジュリア・ライ／ダヴィッド・サヴォルド編　晶文社刊）という本を読みました。この本には50項目くらいの謎があり、その中に『同じ形の雪の結晶はあるのか』という項目があげてありました。数100万年前から降り続いている雪の結晶は、全部違う……ということです。

ひと目でわかる水の評価方法はないか

それまでに私は、なんとか水の違いを表わす方法はないものかと、悩んでいましたから、『ああ、これだ！』と思いつきました。

誰もがパッとひと目見てわかるような、水の評価方法はないか……。

そんなところから考え出したのが『水の氷結結晶（以下結晶という）写真』です。この方法なら、知りたい水を凍らせてできる結晶を、写真に撮影すればいいのです。

水を凍らせて、その結晶を撮影したら、その水の情報が得られるのではないか……と考えたのです。

苦労を重ねた末に、結晶写真を撮影し、拡大してスライドにすることができました。そして講演などに持って行くと、その美しさと不思議さに、コピーを頼まれることも多くなったのです。結晶写真の美しさと醜さが人を引き付けてくれました。

そのようなことが重なって、結晶写真に対する喜びと、神秘さをわかちあいたいという切なる願いから、この本の出版を企画しました。

Introduction

Masaru Emoto, Water and HADO, which signifies the world of subtle energy related to consciousness, synonymous with "Chi" in Japanese

My encounters with the study of water when I became acquainted with Dr. Lee H. Lorenzen. Dr. Lorenzen was at that time 34 while I was 41. Dr. Lorenzen studied biochemistry at the University of California at Berkley and later became a water researcher, developing "micro-cluster water" (or Magnetic Resonance Water).
Since the encounter with Dr. Lorenzen, I had become attracted to the study of water and had begun wanting to know more about the properties of water. I wondered if there were any machines that could measure and see water. It was at this time that through Dr. Lorenzen, I encountered a machine that could measure HADO, called an MRA, Magnetic Resonance Analyzer. It was after this discovery that my research started to advance with increasing speed.

The MRA was used at that time in the USA for homeopathy (a popular drug therapy in Germany). The minute that I saw this machine, an idea flashed through my mind that it could be used in the study of "micro-cluster water" (Magnetic Resonance Water), so I brought it back to Japan as an instrument that could hopefully contribute to my research.

As a result, "HADO water" that transcribes HADO information by MRAs in micro-cluster water, that Dr. Lorenzen produced at my request, demonstrated that the physical condition of people can be improved by water.

I have introduced the use of the MRA and HADO in my literary works as listed below. Please refer to them for specific details.

"The Prelude to the HADO Age" Sun Road publishing Co., Ltd.
"Human Science of HADO" Business Publishing Co., Ltd.
"Truth of 'HADO' Theory" PHP Institute, Inc.
"The Study of Water and Life from the Viewpoint of 'HADO' Science" PHP Institute, Inc.
"Food Science of HADO" Co-author, Akiko Sugahara Takanawa Publishing Co., Ltd.
"Happiness in Hard Times" Co-author, Ravi Batra PHP Institute, Inc.
"Saving Our World. The 'HADO' Theory Revolution" PHP Institute, Inc.
"'HADO' Theory Gives New Meaning to Human Happiness" PHP Institute, Inc.
"HADO: Tuning into a New Reality" PHP Institute, Inc.
"What is HADO?" PHP Institute, Inc.
"Awakening Latent Memory - In Search of a New Self" PHP Institute, Inc.

As I began doing more research on water, I became interested in taking pictures of various frozen water crystals. Through these pictures, I have gained a great experience by seeing these faces of water. These pictures were so wonderful that I just had to show them, so I decided to edit them into this picture book, "The Message from Water".

Water, Humans and Earth

A human being appears on this earth physically for the first time when an ovum of the mother and sperm of the father meet each other and become a fertilized egg. At this time water accounts for about 95% of the fertilized egg, in other words, it is almost all water. The amount of water in a matured human body is 70%. No wonder it is said that the human body is made of water.

People live their lives surrounded by various kinds of water everyday until the day they die.

The earth is called the "Water Planet" and about 70% of its surface is covered with water. Isn't this somewhat similar to the human body? Most of the planet's water such as rainwater, underground water, lakes, marshes and rivers is in the sea. Some water floats in the air in the form of clouds or mist. Firn in high mountains and ice in Antarctic are also originally water.

As I went on with my research of water, I became unsure whether the precious water that I am working with was clean water or unclean water, or subsequently what it means to the human body. No one except for a water research institution or water research professionals really know the definite answer. Water, whatever it's makeup, appears the same to our eyes.

What is the difference in the information that each kind of water holds? Is there any possible way of seeing that?

While I was thinking about this, I came across a book titled, "THE DAY THAT LIGHTNING CHASED THE HOUSEWIFE" (Edited by Julia Leigh and David Savold, Shobun-sha Publisher). This book contains about 50 questions. Among them, there was a question that asked "Are there any snow crystals of the same shape?" The answer was that snow has been falling on earth for a few million years and each crystal has a different shape.

Can You Make Evaluations of Water in a Glance?

I had always wondered if there were methods of expressing the difference of water nature. And that was when it hit me that "This is it!"

That was what led me to make these "pictures of frozen crystals of water" (hereafter referred to as crystals). With this method, all I had to do was to take pictures of the crystals made by freezing water."

If I freeze water and take a picture of the crystals that form, I could obtain information about the water. That was the whole idea behind the experiment that I was about to start.

I enlarged my pictures of crystals into slides and brought them to my lectures. Since then, I started to get requests for copies of them because of their beauty and mysteriousness. The loveliness as well as ugliness of the crystal pictures attracted people. It was from these events and my earnest desire to share the joy and mysteriousness of crystals that I decided to publish this book.

第一章 身近な水の話

水と環境問題

地球上を循環する水、地球上にある水の量などを考えるとき、環境問題が浮かびあがってきます。

環境問題では、水の汚染をどう防ぐか、あるいは水をどう浄化するかということが、非常に大きな問題になってきます。水はこの地球上でつねに限りなく循環し、すべての汚染を吸収し、溶かしこんでしまうからです。

水は命の源です。この水が汚れてしまったら、すべての生き物はその存在を否定されてしまうのです。こんなことからも、1日も早く、水の評価を明らかにする方法はないかと考え続けていました。

地球上の水は大丈夫でしょうか

そして、私たちがふだん何気なく使っている水道水も、いろいろな姿をしている「水」のひとつです。

水道水の、直接的な源は河川です。川の水が浄水場に集められ、塩素などを使って殺菌・消毒され、水道管を通って各家庭に運ばれています。

そして都会では、その水道水に「浄水器」をつけることも一般的になりました。都会の「水」が汚染されているのです。それは、どの程度の汚染なのでしょうか。もともとの川の水汚染が原因でしょうか。それとも家庭の蛇口までの間の、どこかで汚染されているのでしょうか。

また自然の湧き水はどんな状態なのでしょう。

もっとさかのぼって、空から降ってくる雨はどうでしょう。雨水は本来、地球の蒸留水のはずですが、大気中の不純物によって汚染されているのでしょうか。

科学的な実験をし、それぞれの水に含まれる不純物や汚染物質を分析してみても、なんだか部分的で、数字の魔術のような感じもします。

私たちの生活にとって欠かすことのできない水ですが、考えてみると、いろいろな疑問がふくれあがります。

東京と大阪では、どちらの水がより汚染されているのでしょう。

北海道や九州など地方都市はどうでしょう。

田舎の水は、本当にきれいなのでしょうか……。

Chapter 1 Story of Water in Daily Life

Water and Environmental Problems

We cannot think about the quantity of water that circulates this earth without thinking about environmental problems. To solve environmental problems we need the prevention of water contamination, resulting in higher purification levels of water. Water circulates in this world limitlessly and absorbs and dissolves all contaminants. Water is the source of life. If water is contaminated, all creatures would be denied of their existence.
Considering these environmental situations, I continued to seek a way to clearly evaluate water.

Can the Water on the Earth Survive?

The tap water that we unconsciously use everyday, is one type of water that has many figures.
Most tap water is directly from rivers. River water is collected in a treatment plant to undergo sterilization and disinfection by chlorine. The water is then transported to each home through water pipes.
It has become common practice for home users in cities to attach a water purifier to the water faucet. Water in most cities is contaminated. How bad is the contamination and is it because the original river water is contaminated? Did it get contaminated on the way to the home water faucets?
How contaminated is natural spring water?
To go further back, how contaminated is the rain that falls from the sky contaminated? Does rainwater get contaminated impurities in the air although it is to be originally distilled on the earth?
Even scientific experiments and analyses of impurities and contaminants contained in each water sample seem to be partially a numeric magic.
Water is essential to our life, but when we think of it, it contains a lot of problems.
Which tap water is more contaminated, Tokyo or Osaka?
How about local cities in Hokkaido and Kyushu?

Is water in the rural areas really more pure?

水という文字は……

水の結晶写真を撮影中、どの氷も写真のような状態を通って水に戻ります。
水が凍って結晶になり、温度が上がって水に戻る寸前の一瞬、−5℃から0℃の間で、「水」という漢字
とそっくりの姿を見せてくれます。昔の人はこのことを知って「水」という文字をつくったのでしょうか。
漢字以外の文字については、この推理は当てはまりませんが……。

While taking pictures of water crystals, whatever kind of ice melts to water through the state shown in the picture.
When water freezes, it becomes crystallized. At the moment right before it returns to it's water form (with a rise in temperature, between -5℃ and 0℃) it creates a shape that is identical to the Chinese character for water. Did people in the ancient times know this and make the Chinese character for "Water" based on this information?
Other letters except Chinese ones may not be applied to this reasoning.

『結晶』は「水の顔」

　結晶とは、原子あるいは分子が規則正しく配列している状態の個体で、雪や水晶のほかに、ダイヤモンドなどの天然の鉱物、食塩、化学調味料などにも結晶が見られます。

　とくに雪は諸条件の重なりによって生まれることから、同じ顔をした結晶はひとつもありません。これは2人として同じ人間がいないことと似ています。

　そして雪ばかりではなく、地球上のいろいろな水にも、独自の結晶構造があるはずだと考えました。

　水の分子が結晶したとき、きれいな水はきれいな結晶をみせる。しかし汚染された水は美しく結晶しないのでは……と、そう思いついたのです。

　1994年、早速実験にかかりましたが、なにしろいろいろな水を凍らせ、小さな壊れやすい結晶を、それも溶けないように顕微鏡のステージに乗せて、超特急で撮影する必要があります。

　まず、凍らせる水の量、シャーレの素材や容量、ドライアイスやクーラーも総動員しました。冷凍庫の庫内温度、冷却時間、実験用の冷蔵室の温度、顕微鏡観察倍率、ライトの当て方、レンズの絞りなど、実にさまざまな条件をひとつずつクリアしてはじめて撮影できます。

　この実験に取り組んでから、満足のいく結晶写真が撮影されるまでに、2ヵ月という時間を要しました。この間、何百、何千枚というフィルムを無駄にしたことでしょう。

　でも、最初に結晶写真を得たときの感動はえもいわれないものがありました。（14ページの写真）

　なんでも最初の1枚が大切な意味をもつものです。

　これに勢いを得て、冷凍庫と、カメラをセットした顕微鏡が入るような大きさの冷蔵室をつくり、そして『結晶写真撮影班』を結成しました。少しずつ写真を増やし、データを蓄積していきました。

Water Crystal Is the Face of Water

Crystal is a solid substance with orderly configured atoms and molecules. In addition to being in snow and crystallized quartz, crystals are also seen in natural minerals such as diamonds, table salt, and chemical seasoning like MSG.

In particular, because snow is formed under a variety of conditions, there are no crystals that have the same face (as is true with people's faces.)

This is due to the fact that for snow flakes to have the same crystal structure, the various types of water on the earth have to start out having the same crystal structures.

I had a theory. When a water molecule crystallizes, pure water becomes pure crystal, but contaminated water may not crystallize as beautifully? Well, at least I thought so.

In 1994, I immediately started my experiment. I needed to get each sample of water frozen. Then before they melted I had to place these small fragile crystals on the microscope stage to be photographed at a super high speed.

First of all, I had to get a full set of equipment: the required quantity of water samples to freeze, Petri dishes which material and volume are considered, dry ice and a cooler. Photographing the crystals could only be possible after meeting various conditions, the exact freezer temperature, specific times to be cooled, exact refrigerator temperature, microscopic observation magnification, how to light the object, and lens iris.

It took about 2 months before I was able to take a picture that I was satisfied with. During this period, I must have wasted a few hundreds or a few thousands of rolls of film.

However, it was a very impressive moment when I succeeded in taking my first picture of a water crystal.(Picture in page 14)

After that initial photograph, my experiment gained momentum. I then made a refrigerated room in which a small freezer and a microscope set with a camera could fit. After organizing a "crystal photographing group" my colleagues and I took pictures one by one and stored the data.

はじめて撮影に成功した結晶写真／マイクロクラスター水
The first successful crystal picture we took/Micro-cluster Water

新しい水の評価法の発見

　水は変化が激しく、不安定なものです。調べたいと思うひとつの試料水を100個のシャーレに滴下し、冷凍庫に２時間入れておきます。できあがってくる結晶を捕え、顕微鏡を通し、200～500倍の倍率で撮影をします。

　しかも、いろいろな結晶の中から平均的なものを得るために、考えられる限りの努力が続きました。

　マイナス５℃に設定した冷蔵庫での撮影は、スタッフの体力を考えると、１回の作業はどうしても30分以内に限られます。

　結晶写真の撮影については、完全に同じ結果、つまり同じ結晶は得られないわけですから、再現性という点では100点満点の結果ではありません。でもたとえば、格子状の結晶が多いとか、板状の結晶が多いなどの、はっきりとした傾向が見られ、傾向性という面では、識別ができていると思っています。74ページに１回に１種類の試料水を100のサンプル用意し、凍らせて撮影したときの、いろいろな結晶写真を掲載しました。美結晶、六角、不定型、結晶なし、などにわかれますが、ある一定の傾向性が見られることがわかります。

　われわれは結晶写真から多くのことを学びました。今までに、企業や有志の方などの協力も得て、世界各地、また、日本中の湧き水、雨水、河川、湖沼の水を凍らせて撮影することができました。

　４年半で約１万枚の写真を撮影、所蔵しています。

　とくにこの写真集にご紹介した海外の水のほとんどは元・ニチレイアイス社長の田口哲也さん（『氷の文化史～人と氷のふれあいの歴史』冷凍食品新聞社刊の著者）が、世界中をくまなく歩いて採水してこられたものです。

Discovery of a New Water Evaluation Method

Water changes rapidly and is unstable. We dropped one sample of water to be tested on 100 Petri dishes and placed them in a freezer for 2 hours. We took the crystals out and put them under the microscope to be photographed at magnifications of 200-500 times.

In order to obtain an example of an average crystal we had to photograph as many samples, under as many conditions as we could think of. It's only physically possible for most people to last about 30 minutes (at the longest) while taking pictures inside a refrigerator set at 5℃ below zero.

It is impossible to obtain identical crystal pictures. In other words, it is impossible to perfectly reproduce the same crystal twice. However, crystals can show a certain distinctive tendency called a grid crystal or laminar crystal structure. Crystals can be identified by this structural tendency. On page 74, there are pictures of crystals taken by freezing 100 samples at a time for 1 type of water. Although there are many examples of crystals in these samples such as beautiful crystals, hexagonal crystals, variable crystals, or no crystal, we can see that there is a certain tendency in all of the samples to form a grid crystal structure.

We learned many things from these pictures of crystals.

Thanks to the cooperation of several companies and volunteers hitherto, we were able to take pictures of spring water, rainwater, river water, lakes and marshes all across the world and in Japan.

We have photographed and stored about 10,000 pictures in 4 and a half years.

Most of the water from overseas shown in this picture collection was collected by Mr. Tetsuya Taguchi, the former President of Nichirei Ice Co., Ltd., who traveled all over the world and wrote "The Cultural History of Ice: Links between Man and Ice," published by the Reitou Shokuhin Journal.

▲冷蔵室／Refrigeration room

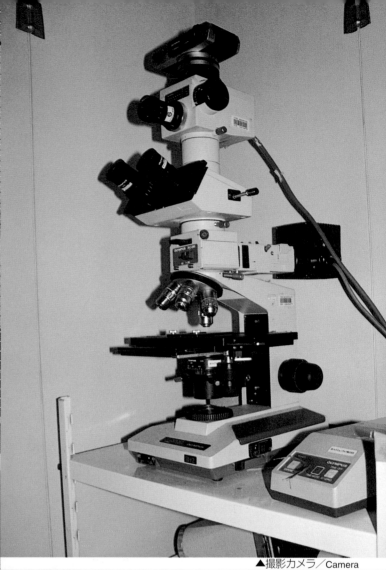

▲撮影カメラ／Camera

▲冷凍庫。1つの試料水を100個のシャーレに分けて、氷結させている様子
Freezer　Water to be tested is divided into 100 Petri dishes for freezing.

▲試料水をスポイトで取り出し、シャーレに1滴落とし、凍らせている様子
Placing a drop of water to be tested into a Petri dish using a pipette.

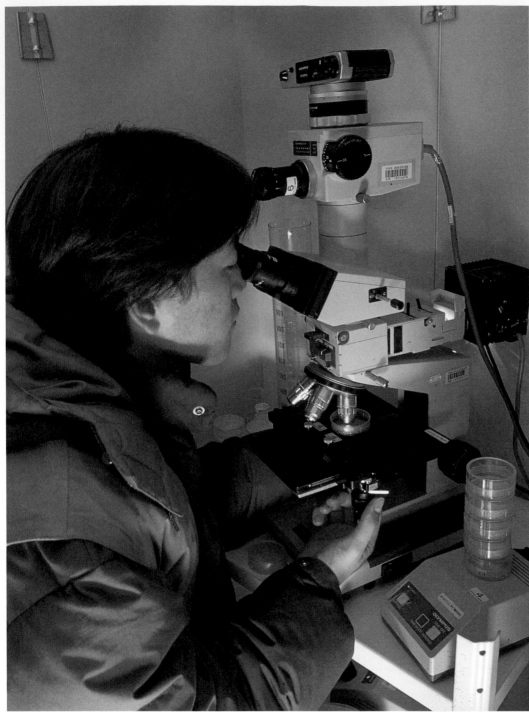

▲−5℃設定の冷蔵庫で撮影している
Photographing inside a refrigeration room set at -5℃

氷の先端部分を撮影している ▶
Photographing the ice tip

水からの伝言

　私たちスタッフが、実際に結晶写真を見るときは、最初の一枚の写真から教えられたように『六角形の整った結晶構造をしているかどうか』がもっとも重要です。経験から、結晶構造の欠けや崩れは、良い徴候ではないと思います。つまり、普通に眺めて、美しいと感じるかどうかが判断の基準です。

　撮影のため、結晶のできる過程を何千回と見てきました。すると不思議なことに、水の「がんばる様子」を見たり感じたりするようになりました。

　そして結晶写真は素晴らしい伝言を運んでいる、水が人間に何かを語りかけていると思いました。

　これらの結晶写真はまさに「水の顔」でした。

　水は基本的には『良い水になろう！　良い水になりたい！』と、けなげに努力していると思います。

　そんな表情が伝わってきたのです。

　水の結晶写真は、現代の科学的な水の分析方法とは少し離れるかもしれません。まったく違った角度からみた、水の評価方法です。

　さらに、水の流れと人の行方と言われるように、水は決して定まることがありません。結晶として撮影されたものは、その日、その時の状態を表わしています。

　従って、これを科学的レベルまで引き上げていくためには、毎日のように、いろいろな所で多くの人々の手によって、観測されなければなりません。

　ともあれ、これはたぶん、世界ではじめての試みです。このような手法において、水にアプローチする方法もあるという提言として、水が見せてくれる「水の顔」に出会ってください。

A Message from Water

When our staff actually looks at the crystal picture, it is most important that they notice that it has a completed "hexagonal crystal structure", as we saw in the first picture. From our experience, we know that the chipping away and/or collapsing of crystal structures are not good signs. In other words, the judgment criteria is whether you can feel that it is beautiful or not by looking at it.

During the photographing, we observed the crystallization process a few thousand times. Then strangely, we came to feel and see the crystal trying to become "beautiful crystal figure" of water, and that crystal pictures carry wonderful messages. We felt that the water was trying to say something to us. We came to understand that these crystal pictures show different "faces of water".

Water, basically, is trying hard, bravely, to be a "Clear water! I want to be clear water!"

We felt such expression coming out from the crystals of water.

Pictures of crystallized water may deviate slightly from the information given by modern scientific water analysis. Our water evaluation method comes at the analysis from a completely different angle.

In addition, as is often quoted, "Flow of people as well as water is not stable." The pictures of the water crystals express the condition of that sample of water only in that very moment of that very day.

Therefore, in order to raise this analysis to a scientific level, the crystals must be observed on a daily basis at various locations and analyzed with many people's supports.

In any case, this is perhaps the first attempt of this kind in the world. We hope you will enjoy this introduction to a unique method of approaching the study of water, called the "Faces of water".

日本の水道水

水道水の結晶写真

現在の日本の上水道水に、塩素や塩素処理によるトリハロメタン、その他環境ホルモンの原因となる化学物質が含まれていることは、残念ながら周知の事実です。実際に大都市の水道水をそのまま飲むと、塩素臭が鼻につくこともあります。

水道水がまずい理由は、水道水となるダムや川などの元の水を、飲めるように殺菌するために消毒薬を加えたから……であることも、おそらく知られています。また「加えられた消毒薬は、人体に影響ありません」と説明されれば、黙ってうなずくしかありません。でも実際には多くの人達が、浄水器を使って有害と思われる物質を取り除き、自分たちの身体を守っているのです。

地方や田舎へ行っても、日本の水道の普及率は、ほぼ100％。現在では地下水や井戸水を汲みあげて、直接飲用している人は本当にわずかです。

それに全国の水道水には、ある一定の基準があり、その基準をクリアしないと広く提供できないことが法律で定められています。

そこで各地の水道水を結晶にして撮影しました。一定の基準を満たしている水道水は、果たして全国どこでも同じような結晶になったのでしょうか。

Tap Water, in Japan.

Picture of Tap Water Crystals

Regretfully, it is a known fact that chlorine, chlorinated tri-halomethane and other chemical substances that are the causes of environmental hormones are found in the tap water of Japan. When we drink the tap water in major cities, we actually smell a chlorine odor.

We all know that this is one of the reasons why the tap water is not good. The water that comes from dams and rivers has disinfectants added to it to make it drinkable. And since it carries a sign saying, "Added disinfectants are not harmful to humans," we are supposed to believe that it is OK. Actually though, many people use water purifiers to remove the seemingly harmful substances that they instinctively know threaten their bodies.

The ratio of waterworks covering local and rural areas is nearly 100% in Japan. These days, only a small amount of people pump underground water or well water to use as drinking water.

There is a specific nationwide standard for tap water, and it is provided for by law that the water that doesn't satisfy these standards cannot be supplied to the public.

I decided to take pictures of tap water samples in there crystal forms. Do tap water samples that satisfy the national standards have the same kind of crystals no matter where the samples are found in Japan?

Sapporo City, Hokkaido
北海道・札幌市

札幌市は大都会ですが、郊外の環境は東京のそれと比べたら、まだまだ自然がそのままに残っています。この札幌市の水道水の水源は豊平川。それほど汚染されている川ではないのですが、水道水ではやはり、きれいな結晶を得ることはできませんでした。
でも、必死でまっとうな結晶になろうと努力しているようにも見えます。

Sapporo is a large city, but when comparing it's suburban environment with the suburbs of Tokyo, the nature is more intact. The water source of the tap water in Sapporo comes from the Toyohira River. Although this river is not polluted as badly as some others, we could not obtain clear crystals from this tap water.
However, it seems that it is trying desperately hard to be a clean water.

Sendai City, Miyagi Prefecture
宮城県・仙台市

「杜の都」、水の美しい街として有名な仙台市ですが、水道水は……。
これもまた、という感じです。

Sendai is famous as the "City of Forests", and it has beautiful water sources. But as for its tap water, it is the same as Sapporo's.

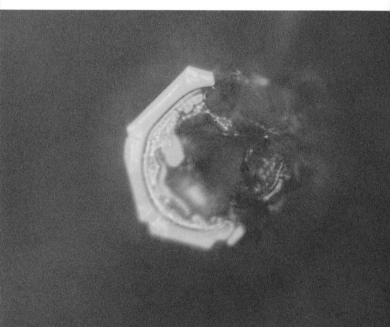

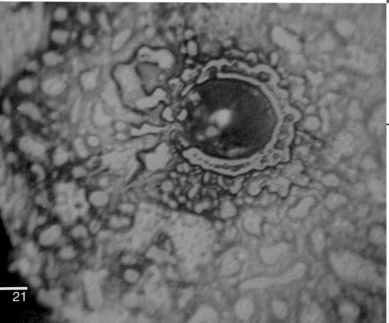

Kanazawa City, Ishikawa Prefecture
石川県・金沢市

北陸の都市で城下町。市内に浅野川、犀川が流れており、市内中央の兼六園は日本三銘庭園のひとつです。
しかし、水道水の結晶は……。

Kanazawa is the largest city in the Hokuriku district and is a castle town. The Asano River and the Sai River flow through the city, and Kenrokuen Park at the center of the city has one of the 3 famous gardens of Japan. However, the water is...

東京都・品川区

予想どおり東京の水は、良くないことを証明してしまったような写真です。
結晶化する予兆も見えません。大都会という環境のなかにある水の宿命なのでしょうか。

This picture seems to indicate that the water in Tokyo is not as good as we had expected.
This picture of Tokyo's tap water shows no sign of crystallization. Is this the fate of water in a metropolitan environment?

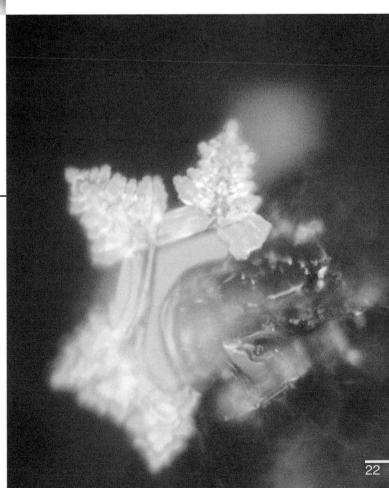

Nagoya City, Aichi Prefecture

愛知県・名古屋市

大都市の水道水としては珍しく、結晶になる一歩手前の姿がとらえられました（木曾川系水源）。
完全な六角形になろうとする水を阻害している要因は、いったいなんでしょうか。

Unexpectedly, we were able to capture its figure just before crystallization, rarely seen in tap water in large cities. The Water source is the Kiso River.
What is the factor that impedes a water crystal from forming a complete hexagon?

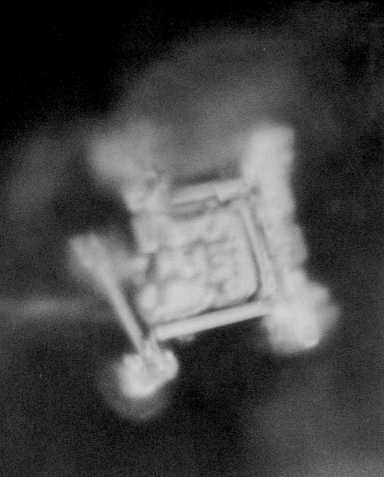

大阪市・北区

大阪も「水の都」……でしたが、今では、水のまずさで定評のある都市に。
ただこの写真、かなりいびつですが結晶になろうとしています。
しかも角には枝も見られ、発展願望が大。

Osaka used to be a "City of Water". But it has become a city famous for unpalatable water.
The sample of water from Osaka seems to be trying to crystallize, though it is significantly distorted. We can see branches at the corners which indicate that it is trying to becoming fully developed.

Katano City, Osaka Prefecture

大阪府・交野市

交野市は大阪市の北部、奈良と京都の県境にあります。
交野市の水道水は、6割を地下水を水源としているためか、とてもきれいな結晶がとれました。
そういえば、千利休がお茶をたてるときに、交野の水をわざわざ取り寄せて使ったとか……。

Katano city lies in the northern part of Osaka and on the prefectural border between Nara and Kyoto.
We were able to obtain a clear crystal from the tap water in Katano, since 60% of it comes from an underground water source. Come to think of it, Sen-no-Rikyu, a tea master and a founder of the Sen school of tea ceremony, used water from Katano to make tea.

Hiroshima City, Hiroshima Prefecture
広島県・広島市

川と橋の町、広島。原爆の洗礼を受けた町、広島。
酒どころとして名高い西条もひかえていて、昔から水のおいしい
ところでした。必死で六角形になろうとしている結晶は、まろや
かな人の優しさと団結を表わしているようです。

Hiroshima, a city of rivers and bridges. Hiroshima, a city baptized by the atomic bomb.
Saijo is famous for it's sake, and the water in this city has always been good since ancient times. The crystal that is trying hard to develop into a hexagon seems to be expressing the graceful kindness and solidarity of its people.

Fukuoka City, Fukuoka Prefecture
福岡県・福岡市

九州一の大都市・福岡。やはり都会の水道水で美しい結晶を得る
のは無理なのでしょうか。
結晶の半分ほどが何かに浸食されたような形ですが、結晶の名残
りは見られます。

The largest city in Kyushu, Fukuoka. Is it an impossible task to try to obtain a clear crystal from a city tap water? About half of the crystals that we photographed seemed to have been eroded by something, but still there are traces.

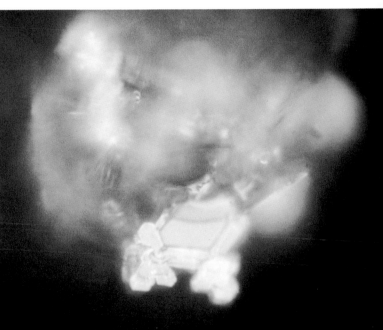

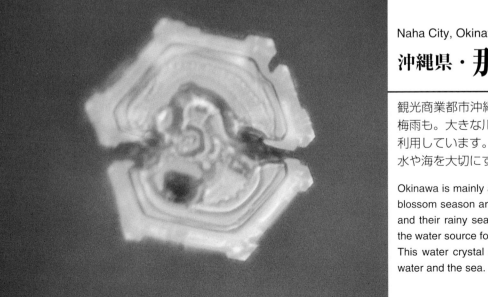

Naha City, Okinawa Prefecture
沖縄県・那覇市

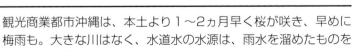

観光商業都市沖縄は、本土より1～2ヵ月早く桜が咲き、早めに
梅雨も。大きな川はなく、水道水の水源は、雨水を溜めたものを
利用しています。
水や海を大切にする人々の気持ちが表わされているようです。

Okinawa is mainly a tourist and commercial city. On the island, the cherry blossom season arrives about 1 to 2 months earlier than on the mainland and their rainy season also comes earlier. There are no large rivers so the water source for their tap water comes from rainwater reservoirs.
This water crystal seems to express the people's warm feelings toward water and the sea.

海外の水道水

世界の水事情

　所変われば品変わる……のたとえにあるように、水ほどその環境（文明、文化を含む）や風土によって変わるものはないでしょう。

　そのため、ＷＨＯ（世界保健機構）では、1984年に水質指針（ガイドライン）を作成しましたが、そのなかで『飲料水の安全判定の目安や処理目標としての基準は、各国がその国内状況（水事情、社会全体の環境レベル、技術力、経済力など）を勘案して決めるべきであり、指針はそのための基礎資料を提供するにすぎない』と注釈しているほどです。

　ですから、水道水の浄水処理方法は、各国によってまちまちなのですが、わが国では、主として塩素を中心とした処理システムが省令によって定められている、ということになります。

　今回、ご紹介する外国の水道水の結晶写真は、紙面の都合で、ロンドン、パリ、ニューヨーク、カナダ、アルゼンチン、ブラジルの6都市だけです。しかし、日本の水道水の結晶写真と比較してみると、案外きれいなものが多いのです。

　その理由は、それぞれの国の原水の汚染度の違い。そして、水の処理システムの違いにあるようです。

Tap Water, Overseas

The Water Circumstances of the World

Each country has its own customs. Nothing else is changed so much by the environment and the natural features of the land (including civilization and culture) as is the water.

For this reason, the WHO (World Health Organization) created water guidelines in 1984. In these guidelines it is stated that "The standard for safety judgment of drinking water and criteria for treatment should be determined by each country giving consideration to its own domestic conditions (water circumstances, environmental level of the entire society, technical as well as economical power) and these guidelines are only provided as a basic material for that purpose." Therefore, the water purification method for tap water differs according to each country. In our country, a treatment system using mainly chlorine has been provided by the ministerial ordinance of each prefecture.

These pictures of tap water crystals from around the world were taken only from 6 large cities: London (UK), Paris (France), New York (USA), Vancouver (Canada), Buenos Aires (Argentina) and Manaus (Brazil). However, when compared with the pictures of Japanese tap water crystals, they were surprisingly more clear.

It seems that the reason is the difference in the degree of contamination of the water sources in each country, as well as the difference in the water treatment systems.

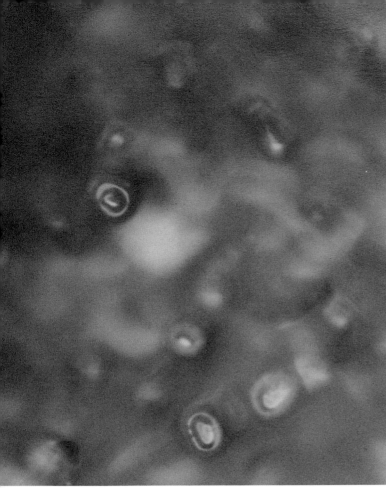

London, UK

イギリス・**ロンドン**

霧の都ロンドンの水道水です。
結晶というには程遠い状態しか得ることはできませんでしたが、
日本の水道水と比べてみると、なんともいえません。

The tap water of London, a foggy city.
We could only obtain crystals that were not fully developed as was frequently the case in Japan.

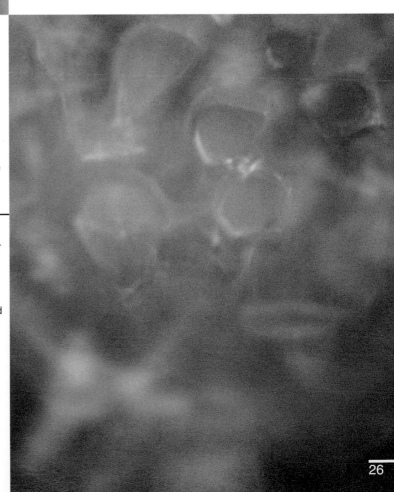

Paris, France

フランス・**パリ**

セーヌ川の流れるパリの水道水です。
なかなか結晶するというにはいたりませんが、思っていたよりひどくはない……といったところでしょうか。

The tap water of Paris where the Seine River flows.
The sample did not crystallize easily but it was not as bad as we had expected.

New York, USA

アメリカ・ニューヨーク

アメリカ大陸の東海岸にあるニューヨークは、人種のるつぼといわれていますが、水道水は日本の湧き水よりいい顔をしているものがあります。
ちなみに、ニューヨークの処理システムはフッ素、オゾン処理が中心ということです。

New York is located on the east coast of the North American Continent and is said to be the melting pot of races.
We can see that some of the top water crystals have better faces than those of Japanese spring water.
In New York, tap water is usually fluorinated or ozonized.

Vancouver, Canada

カナダ・バンクーバー

アメリカ大陸西海岸、すぐお隣りはアメリカのシアトル。
比較的暖かく住みやすいことから、日本人も多く住んでいます。
水道水にしては美しい結晶を保持しています。

Vancouver is located on the west coast of the North American Continent. Seattle, Washington in the USA is just a few miles south from there.
Because the weather is relatively warm and subsequently affords it's population a comfortable living climate, many Japanese people live in Vancouver. The crystals of the water here retained a beautiful crystalline shape especially for those of tap water.

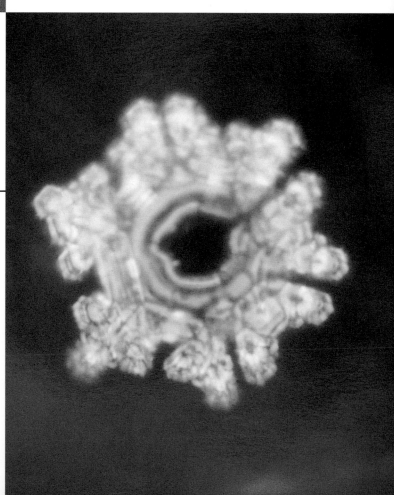

Buenos Aires, Argentina

アルゼンチン・ブエノスアイレス

美しい結晶をみせてくれました。
こんな結晶写真が撮れると、日本の水道水の質の悪さが思われてなりません。
しかし、旅先で飲んで安全かどうかは、また別の問題です。

The water here shows a beautiful crystal shape.
Pictures of these beautiful crystals remind us of how bad the Japanese tap water is.
Beautiful crystals, however, are one thing and safe drinking water while traveling is another.

Manaus, Brazil

ブラジル・マナウス

とても美しい結晶です。
美しく結晶する、水道水が飲める国の人々がうらやましい気がしますが、しかし、消毒基準が日本に比べて、それほど厳しくはないということですので、何とも言えません。

Very beautiful crystals.
The water crystallized beautifully. The people who live in countries where the tap water is drinkable are really very fortunate, but the disinfection criteria are not so exacting as those in Japan.

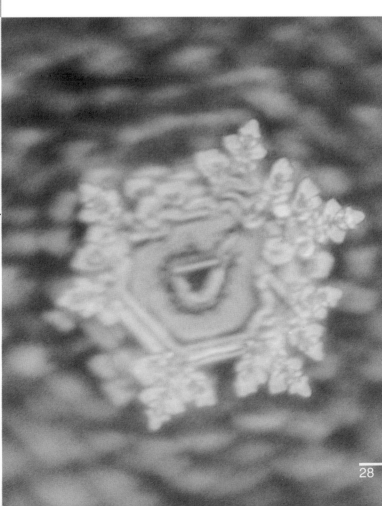

自然界の水

滔々と……が水の自然な姿

「自然水」といいますが、どこからどこまでが「自然」なのか、その境界線はあいまいです。

「人間の影響が及んでいない水」といいかえれば、もはや地球上には「自然水」など残っていないかもしれません。

水は私たち人類が生まれるずっと以前から、地球上に存在していました。そして水は、自然に、滔々と、循環するというサイクルを繰り返していました。

私たちは、その循環していた「自然」の水をちょっと拝借しているだけではなかったのでしょうか。

ちょっとお借りしていたつもりが、生活が便利になり、文化が発展すると同時に、あまりにもたくさんの水を使うようになり、その水を汚し続けることになってしまったよ

うです。そして自分たちで汚した水を「浄化」と称して塩素を入れて消毒し、「不自然」な水をつくり出してしまったのではないでしょうか。

循環する水の浄化力

水は本来、自然なものです。水自身には、自然に自分を浄化する自浄作用がありました。

たとえば雨水が地面に染み込んで、地下水となる過程でろ過されることや、川や湖から蒸発して雲になることも浄化の一種です。シジミ、ハゼ、ボラなどの川と海の間で生きる生き物は、川の上流から流れてきたものを食べて生きています。だから河川は中流とくらべて、河口近くの水がなんとなく美しい結晶を見せてくれることも、自然の浄化といえるのではないでしょうか。

Water in the Natural World

Water Flows Swiftly... is a Natural Figure of Water

We say "natural water", but to what degree is the word "natural" applied? In other words, the boundaries of the word natural are very vague. If we say that water "not influenced by humans" is natural water, then there may be no water left on earth that can be called natural.
Water existed on the earth long before humans emerged. It has repeated its swift circulation cycle naturally.
We were only borrowing circulating "natural" water.
We were just borrowing it, but because it became so convenient, we started using too much water as our human culture developed. As a result, we started polluting water before we put it back in circulation. This polluted water is then "disinfected" with chlorine, which we call purification, whereby creating "unnatural" water.

Purifying Power of Circulating Water

Water is originally natural and has the power to purify itself. For instance, when rainwater penetrates the ground, it is filtered through the soil and becomes part of an underground water source. Water also is filtered when evaporating from rivers and lakes to become clouds in the sky. These are just some of it's natural processes of purification.
Creatures that live between the river and the sea, such as corbicula, goby and striped mullet, eat their food that is carried from upstream. Therefore, it can be said that as a result of this natural purification, the water near the river mouth would show beautiful crystals as compared to the water found mid-stream.

自然水はどこに？

大自然の循環サイクルの中では、つねに大きく浄化作用が働いているようです。

しかし現代では人類の営みのために、大量の農薬や化学肥料、各種の化学物質が土壌に染み込んでおり、雨水はそこをろ過装置として通過しています。したがって地下水や湧き水も汚染されていることになります。

また下水施設や生活雑廃水、工場廃液などを引き受けている河川の汚染はいうまでもなく、自動車の排気ガスや工場が吐き出す煤煙、産業廃棄物などのゴミを焼却する煙も汚染源ですし、原子力発電所もたくさんできています。

あらゆる状況下で汚染された大気。その大気の中を落ちてくる雨水も「酸性雨」となって、人間の汚染を受けています。

また湖や沼も大きく人の手が加わって、せき止められたり、埋め立てられたり、フタをされたり、つぶされたり、引っ越しまでさせられることもあります。

やはり、今や本当の意味での「自然水」を探すことは少なからず努力を要します。

この項では、一般的に『できるだけ人の手が加わっていない状態の水』として、日本国内を中心に、代表的な自然の湧き水や河川・湖沼の水、雨水などをとりあげ、その結晶写真を集めました。

Where Can You Find Natural Water?

Amidst the great circulation cycle of nature, purification is always happening on a large scale. However, today, due to the work of humans, a large amount of chemical substances have penetrated the soil through which rainwater filters. This means that underground water sources and spring water also are contaminated.

Not to mention the contamination that occurs when rivers take in waste water from sewage treatment facilities and plants, gray water, exhaust gas from automobiles, soot and smoke from plants and smoke from incinerating daily industrial waste materials are also contamination sources as well as many nuclear power plants that are being built.

Air is polluted under all kinds of conditions. Rainwater as "acid rain" is also subject to pollution by humans.

Lakes and marshes have been artificially reformed by damming, reclamation, covering, dissipating and even being forced to move.

It indeed requires effort to find "natural" water in the true sense of the word.

In this chapter, we will show a collection of pictures of the water crystals found in typical natural springs, rivers, lakes, marshes and finally in rainwater.

Most of the samples are mainly gathered in Japan as "water not polluted by human hands."

き水

湧き水の自然な顔

日本全国から寄せられる湧き水の撮影は、非常に楽しいものです。

いくら撮影を続けても、さんたんたる状況に陥ってしまう水道水の結晶写真の結果とは、比べものにならないほど、ワクワクドキドキさせられます。

日本は国土の8割が山々におおわれています。先進国としては希少なほど自然の山林も多く残っていて、雨量も豊富で、清浄な水に恵まれた国なのです。

おかげで全国の至るところに湧き水も多く、古くから庶民の暮らしと密接に結びついていました。

しかし戦後の急速な都市開発と山林の人工的整備などにより、汚染のため使えなくなったり、枯渇してしまった湧き水もたくさんあります。

ところが最近になって、水道水の危険性が叫ばれ出し、「ミネラルウォーター」ブームなどともあいまって、自然の湧き水に再びスポットが当たっています。

雑誌などの特集で『名水百選』が取り上げられ、その名水を求めて、何時間もかけて水を汲みに行く人もいます。

全国で自然に湧き出ている水や地下水の中から選んだ結晶写真です。

さて自然の湧水たちは、どんな顔をして、どんなメッセージを伝えてくれるでしょうか。

Spring Water

The Natural Face of Spring Water

These Photographs of spring water collected from all across Japan are very interesting.
Photographing was thrilling especially when compared with the depression that we felt while taking the pictures of the tap water crystals.
Mountains cover about 80% of Japan. Because of this we have an abundance of the natural mountains and forests not commonly seen in industrialized countries. We have plenty of rain and are blessed with pure water.
Since ancient times, this environment and our many natural springs have been closely related with the long and healthy life span of our rural people.
However, with rapid urban development and artificial development of mountains and forests, increased water supply accesses and drainage systems were built after World War II. Because of this, many sources of spring water became unusable due to contamination or due to simply drying up.
But recently, the community was alerted to the dangers of tap water and this (triggering a "mineral water" boom) has caused natural spring water to again draw attention.

"Selected 100 Water of Japan" has been featured in magazines. To seek such water sources, some people travel hours to the identified locations. These are pictures of selected natural spring water crystals.

Now, what kind of faces do the natural spring water and ground water have and what message do they convey?

Ryusendo Cave, Iwate Prefecture

岩手県・竜泉洞

120メートルの深さをもつ地底湖もある、鍾乳洞の近くに湧き出す水。
一部が欠けてはいるものの、大きな力強さを感じます。地底湖の水は浸食されつつも必死で自然を守ろうとしているよう。手遅れにならないうちに、地球をきれいに……と思います。

Water comes springing out near a limestone cave that holds an underground lake as deep as 120 meters in some places.
Although the crystal that is formed from this water is partially chipped, we feel a dynamic strength coming from its structure. The water from the underground lake seems to try to desperately preserve it's uncontaminated nature even if eroded. We believe that we must make the earth beautiful again, before it is too late.

Sanbu-ichi Yusui Spring Water, Nagasaka-cho, Kita-Koma-gun, Yamanashi Prefecture

山梨県北巨摩郡長坂町・三分一湧水

八ヶ岳の雪解け水を源とする「三分一湧水」からは、美しい結晶を得ることができました。
均整のとれた六角形構造をベースに、それぞれの角から三本の枝が別々に伸びている様子は、湧き
水をめぐってみんなが仲良く手をつないでいるように見えます。

From a sample that was made up of Sanbu-ichi Yusui spring water we were able to obtain a beautiful crystal. It is made up of snow water from Mr. Yatsugatake.
Based on a well-balanced hexagonal structure, 3 branches stretch out from each edge of the crystal. This gives the impression of people holding hands together around the spring water.

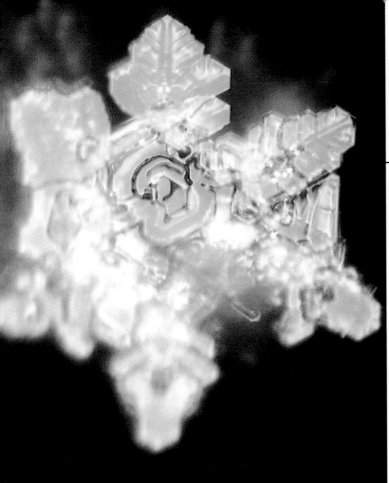

Clear Water of Kobo, Kanagawa Prefecture

神奈川県・弘法の清水
こうほう

弘法大師由来のこの湧き水は、どんな日照りの年にも、枯れることがないといわれています。
観光センターなどで売られている商品は、酒やソバをはじめ、どれも名水をうたってあります。
結晶写真は、地下から湧き上がってくるような力強さを感じます。
素晴らしい宝物を後世に残したいですね。

Originating from Kobo Daishi, this spring is said to never dry up even during a severe draught year.
The products sold at the local tourist centers, including sake and soba, advertise that they are made using water from this spring.
In looking at the picture of the crystal we feel a strong power that seems to come springing out from underground.
We do wish to hand down wonderful treasures to our future generations.

Kobo Spring Water, Fukuyama City, Hiroshima Prefecture

広島県福山市・弘法の湧水
こうほう

1200年ほど前、中国地方を巡っていた弘法大師が、奇病に悩む民衆を救済しようと杖で岩盤を打って湧き出したという水。
弘法の水という名前は、大師の全国行脚中に湧き出したという言い伝えとともに、いろいろな場所に残っています。

2種類の弘法の水はとてもよく似ています。
スタッフもときどき間違えるほどです。

About 1,200 years ago, the great Buddhist teacher Kobo was travelling in the Chugoku region of Japan. There were many people in the region afflicted by a strange illness and to help them, Kobo hammered away the base rock with his staff in order to get at the natural water flowing underneath. This water was named Kobo Spring Water.
The name "Kobo Spring Water" is found in various places throughout Japan, where-ever natural hot waters sprang forth during Kobo's travels.

There are two very similar types of Kobo Spring Water. They are so similar that even our staff sometimes have trouble telling them apart.

Rumbling Water in Tenkawa Village, Yoshino-gun, Nara Prefecture

奈良県吉野郡天川村・ゴロゴロの水

山岳信仰と厳しい修行で名高い大峯山^{おおみねさん}の登山道入り口にあり、鍾乳洞に湧き出る水の音がゴロゴロ
という音をたてて、反響することからこの名前がついています。
洞窟から湧き出る神秘の水といわれています。

This name comes from the rumbling echoing sound that this spring makes. The spring lies in a limestone cave
at the entrance of a mountain path in the Omine Mountains. The people of these mountains are famous for their
worshipping practices and strict ascetic beliefs.
The water that gushes from the mouth of this cave spring is called mystic water for this reason.

Spring Water of Saijo, Hiroshima Prefecture

広島県・西条の湧水

標高500〜700メートルくらいの高地周辺に広がった町は、水が美味しいことから酒どころとしても名高く、兵庫の灘、京都の伏見と並ぶ酒どころです。中心部分までしっかりと結晶しており、周囲にすき間無く広がった枝は見事です。

This town that sprawls in the highlands mountains 500 to 700 meters above sea level is famous as a sake brewing area because of its good water. It is as famous for sake as Nada in Hyogo Prefecture and Fushimi in Kyoto are. The crystal that this spring water forms is firm through the center and branches magnificently. It then spreads out fully leaving no empty space.

Ubuyama's Water, Kumamoto Prefecture

熊本県・産山の水
うぶやま

熊本県の北の端、大分県に接している地で、阿蘇山の北のふもとにある湧水です。
牧畜の盛んな町で、大野川の源流あたりにある名水百選のひとつ。
美しい結晶はひっそりと咲いた、花のよう……。

Ubuyama's water is a spring located at the northern end of Kumamoto Prefecture, which borders Oita Prefecture and lies at the foot of the Aso Mountain where cattle breeding is prosperous. It is also the home of the source of the Ono River, one of the "Selected 100 Waters of Japan".
This beautiful crystal is just like a delicate flower blossom.

Fountain in Lourdes, France

フランス・ルルドの泉

『聖ルルドの泉』は奇跡の泉といわれ、世界中から毎年400万人以上の人が集まります。
愛の波動をもつ水、恨みを逆転させる水として有名です。
集団意識としての良さを表わす……神秘的な輝きが感じられる不思議な結晶です。

"St. Lourdes' Fountain" is said to be a fountain of miracles. The water has HADO from love and it reverses hatred to love. More than 4 million people from every corner of the earth come to visit each year.
This crystal expresses the merits of the collective consciousness. A mysterious crystal that gives off the feeling of mystical glory.

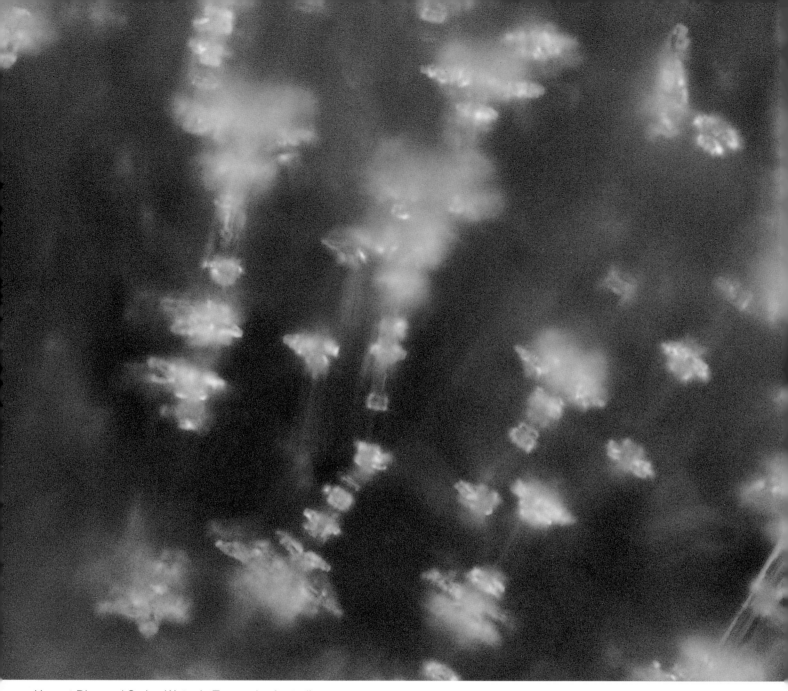

Hogget Diamond Spring Water in Tasmania, Australia

オーストラリア タスマニア　ホグト・ダイヤモンド湧水

オーストラリアの南東部のタスマニア地方は、古生代岩石地帯に属していて、オパールや工業用ダイヤモンドの採取が盛んだった場所。
キラキラと光るダイヤモンドのような結晶がとれたのも不思議です。

The Tasmania region is located at the south eastern end of Australia. The spring is located in a Paleozoic era rock formation where opal and diamond mining (for industrial use) once prospered.
It is no wonder that glittering crystals of diamonds were there.

Underground Water in Northern Island, New Zealand

ニュージーランド北島・地下水

海岸では海水浴、山に登るとスキーができるという、日本人が大好きな旅行地のひとつです。
人の数より羊の数の方が多い国の地下水は、伝統を大切にする人々に守られ、受け継がれているようです。

This is one of the most popular tourist attractions for Japanese people.　The climate is such that while the sea-coast offers warmth enough for swimming, the mountain provide the temperatures needed for skiing.　The underground water of the country where the number of sheep exceed the number of people, is preserved and taken over by people who cherish tradition.

Horobetsu River, Hokkaido

北海道・幌別川

北海道の中央から南へ、日高山脈の山すそから、海にそそぐ幌別川。美しい結晶はまるで花びらのよう……。日本にも、まだまだこんなに美しい結晶を見せてくれる川が残っていることに、改めて感謝したい気持ちです。

This river flows from central Hokkaido southwardly, through the foothills of the Hidaka Mountain range, on to the Horobetsu River and eventually into the sea. These beautiful crystals look just like flower petals.
I am impressed that there is a river still remaining in Japan that has so beautiful crystals.

Goshikinuma, Fukushima Prefecture

福島県・五色沼

^{ばんだい}
磐梯高原の入り口に点在する沼で、水面の色が朱、藍、緑など五色に変わることから、この名前がついています。水面の色の変化は、沼の底にたまった沈殿物と、太陽光線の作用によるものと思われます。雪解けの季節の水の結晶は美しく輝くようです。

The name originated from the look of the water's surface in the dotted marshes at the entrance of the Bandai Plateau. The surface of the water there can be seen by changing into 5 colors ranging from red and blue to green.
This change in color is thought to be affected by the deposits from the marsh bottom combined with the effects of solar rays. A water crystal glitters beautifully during the spring snow melting season.

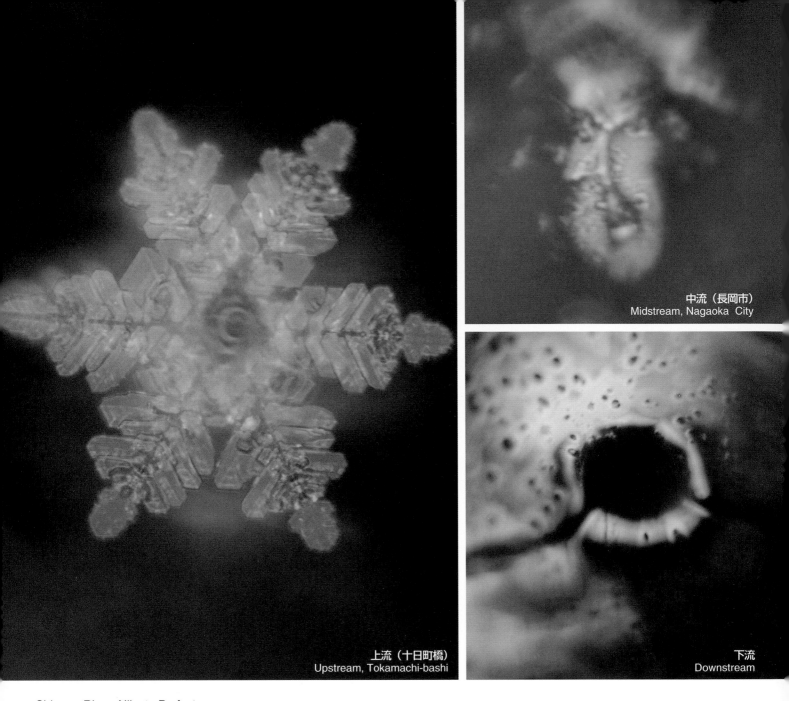

中流（長岡市）
Midstream, Nagaoka City

上流（十日町橋）
Upstream, Tokamachi-bashi

下流
Downstream

Shinano River, Niigata Prefecture

新潟県・信濃川

長野県や新潟県をまたいで流れる信濃川の、上流、中流、下流の結晶写真です。
都市部に入ると、少しずつ汚染されていることがよくわかります。

Pictures of the water crystals found upstream, midstream and downstream in the Shinano River as it flows across Niigata prefecture and Nagano prefecture.
You can see by the crystals, that the river gradually gets contaminated as it flows into an urban area.

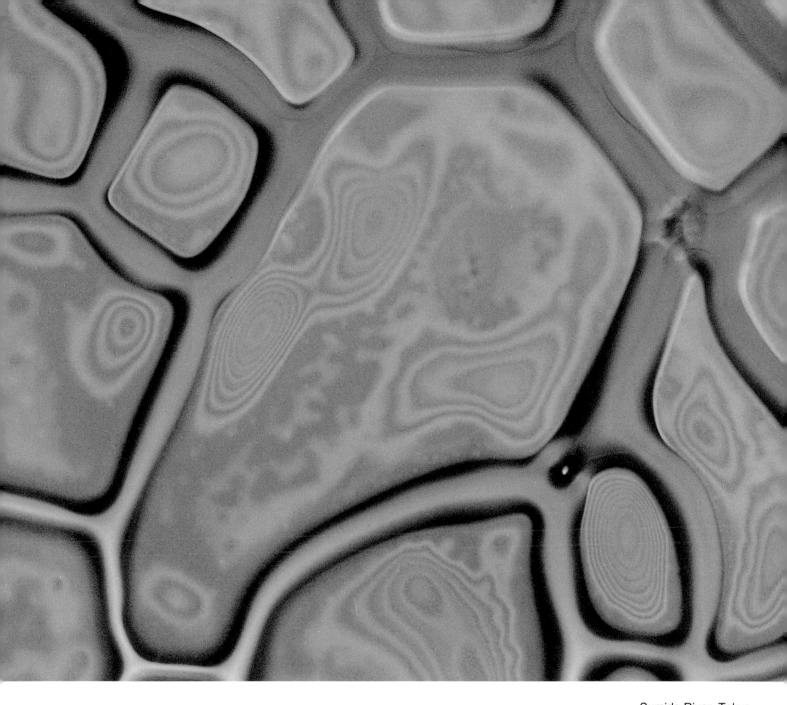

Sumida River, Tokyo
東京都・隅田川

隅田川のほとりにはたくさんの桜が咲いて、人々が集まります。その桜の下を流れる川の本当の顔が、こんなふうだったら……ちょっと悲しいですね。何とも……という感じですが、川そのものは20〜30年前よりはきれいになっています。

Cherry blossom trees bloom along the Sumida River attracting many people.
The actual crystallized face of the river water that flows beneath the cherry blossom trees, looks like this. Isn't it a little bit sad?
It is hard to say such a thing because it has actually become more beautiful now than 20 or 30 years ago.

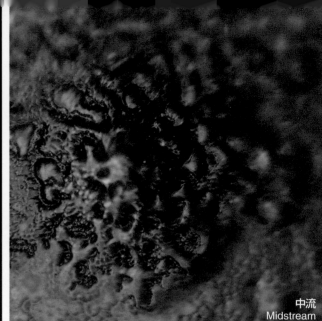

中流
Midstream

上流源水／女取湧水
Upstream/Metori Yusui Spring Water

河口
Mouth of river

Fuji River, Shizuoka Prefecture
静岡県・富士川

富士川は中流域に大きな街があり、やはり汚染されているようです。
ところが、河口付近ではおそらくその辺りに住む魚介類などの浄化作用によって、きれいな水の結晶になっています。水自身も、海に帰るときには美しい姿で……という意志があるようです。

There is a large city at the mid-stream points of the Fuji River, but that area also seems to be contaminated.
But the water crystals found at the rivers mouth are clear because of the purifying affects of the fish and shells living in the vicinity.
This water crystal gives the appearance of having the intention of going back to the beautiful sea.

Ado River, Shiga Prefecture

滋賀県・安曇川
あ　ど　がわ

滋賀県の比良山から、北へ流れて、琵琶湖にそそぐ川。伝統民芸・京扇子の産地でもある高島の街を通過しています。美しい結晶は、日本古来の伝統工芸を守りながら……。
でもこれが、琵琶湖に注いだ後には、どうなるのでしょう。

The Ado river flows northward from Hira Mountain in Shiga Prefecture to the Biwako Lake.
The river passes through the town of Takashima which is the production center of Kyosen, Japanese traditional fan of folk crafts. The beautiful crystal keeps the traditional work craft of Japan.
How will this crystal's form change once it pours into the Biwako Lake?

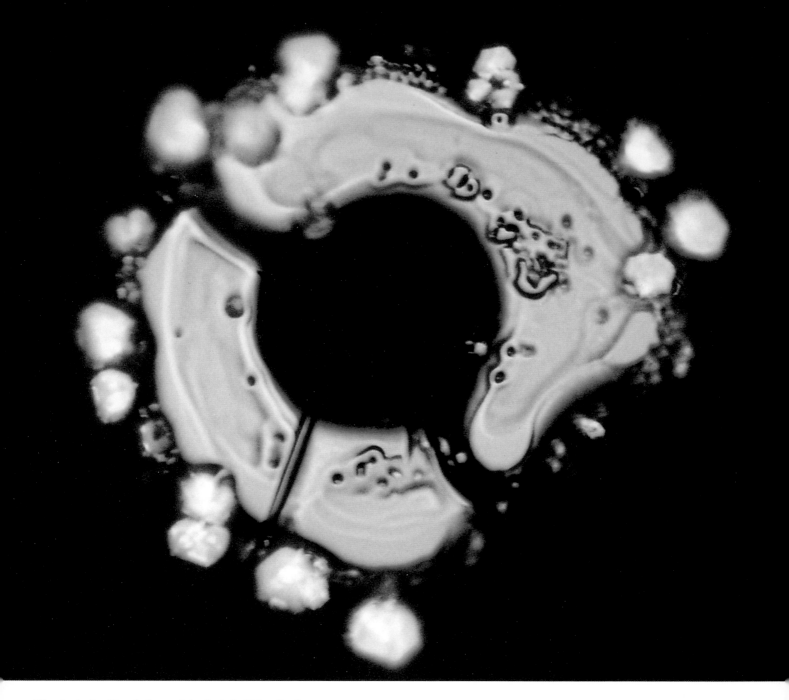

Biwako Lake (South Area of the Lake), Shiga Prefecture

滋賀県・琵琶湖（湖南）

近畿の水がめ。日本の中心にある最大の湖、琵琶湖の水は残念ながら、このような状態です。滋賀県は早くから、県ぐるみで合成洗剤の使用中止を呼びかけるなどの努力をしていますが、それでも琵琶湖の汚染は年々進んでいることを裏付ける、痛ましい姿の写真です。

The largest lake at the center of Japan and the water pool of the Kinki Region. Regretfully, the water of Biwako Lake seems to be like this. This crystal's structure supports the fact that the contamination of Biwako Lake is getting worse each year. This is the case, even though Shiga Prefecture has for many years been making efforts in it's campaign against the usage of synthetic detergents. This is a picture of the water crystal's lamentable figure.

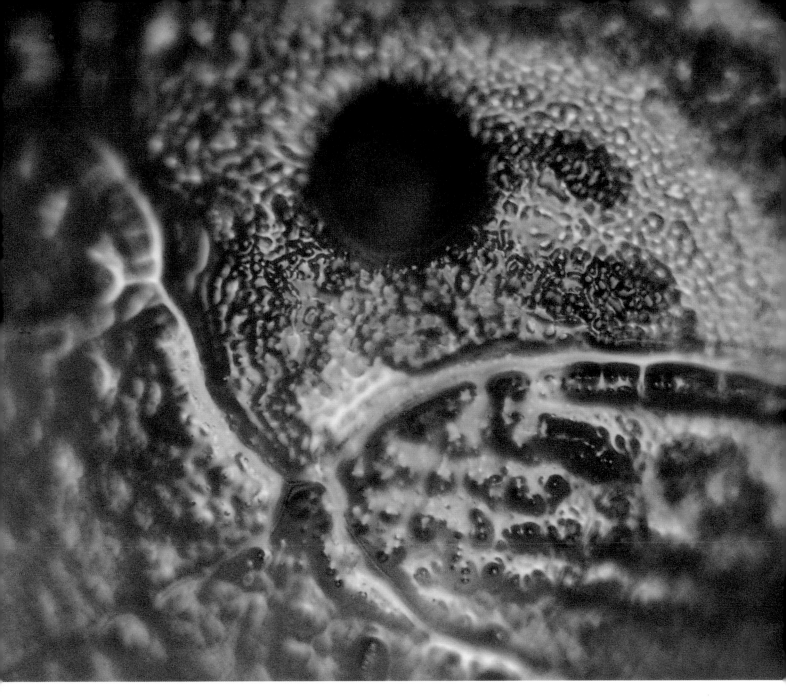

Yodo River, Osaka Prefecture
大阪府・淀川

近畿の平野全体を、ゆったりとうるおしながら南下し、大阪湾にそそぐ淀川。
関西の主要な街々を通り、文字どおり生活全体を洗い流すような役目を負って流れてきた川。生活や人間関係の汚染をも抱えて、苦悩しているのかもしれません。

The Yodo River pours into the Bay of Osaka as it flows southward enriching the entire Kinki plain.
The river passes through most of the major cities in Kansai and flows as if it literally has been given as the role of a general cleaning in its path. It must be suffering with the load of contamination accumulated from its daily life and all of the people that it touches.

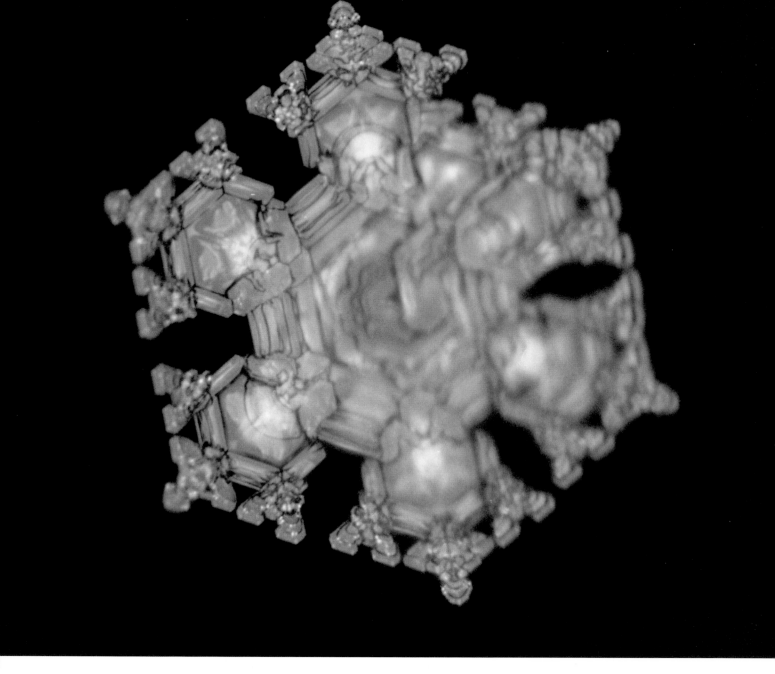

Shimanto River, Kochi Prefecture (Midstream)

高知県・四万十川（中流）

日本最後の清流と呼ばれる四万十川。美しい結晶で枝の部分に特徴があります。
ベースの六角構造の外側に六角形の枝が付き、その先からさらに小さな枝が伸びています。
中流でもこのような美しい結晶がとれますから、水を守ろうとする周辺住民の心意気を感じます。

The Shimanto River is referred to as the last clean stream in Japan. It creates a beautiful crystal which features in the branches.

At the outside of the basic hexagon structure, a hexagon branch is attached and from its edge another small branch stretches out.

This beautiful crystal was taken from the mid section of the river. Within its structure we can feel the spirit of citizens that lived along the river.

氷河・氷層の結晶にロマンを

　地球上の氷は大きく分けて陸にある氷と、海にある氷の2種類があります。氷河とは、陸にある氷のうち、湖や河、凍った土の中にあるもの以外で、雪が降って長い間溜まって凍った氷のことをいいます。なかでも山の中腹にあって、とくに河のように見えるものを氷河と呼んでいます。

　冬になって、雪が降り積もっては、また暖かくなって溶け出したところに、冬がくる……といったことを繰り返し、普通は数年以上、雪の量の少ない地方では100年以上もたって、万年雪の状態になっています。

　高原氷河、山地氷河、谷間氷河、懸垂氷河、山麓氷河などいろいろな姿形をしています。

　氷河は歴史をもっています。

　また氷河には『地層』と同じように『氷層』があります。いつかこれを取り出して、古代の地球の水の結晶を写真に撮って、調べてみたいという、大きなロマンを持っています。

　ここに載せた氷河の水の結晶写真は表面から採取したもので、現在の地球環境の影響を受けているものと思われます。

Glacier

A Dream of Crystal of Glacier and Ice Stratum

Ice on the earth can be divided into roughly two types: ice on the land and ice on the sea. A glacier is located on land, located at places other than lakes, rivers, and frozen soil. A glacier forms from snow that has accumulated over a long period of time. Among glaciers in many places, one that locates at the middle slope of a mountain and that appears like a river is called glacier.

In the winter, snow accumulates rapidly into large piles that will become glaciers. Before the temperature becomes higher and starts to melt the snow, winter comes again. With the repetition of this cycle, normally, in more than a few years the glaciers turn to ice. For regions with little snow fall it takes more than 100 years for a glacier to form. Glaciers are labeled by where they occur geographically; such as, plateau glaciers, mountain glaciers, valley glaciers, suspension glaciers and mountain foot glaciers.

Glaciers have history. Glaciers have ice stratums in the same way that geological formations do. I have this big dream of taking a sample of these stratum some day so as to survey these ancient water crystals.

The pictures of glacial water crystals shown here are of those samples taken from the surface of the glaciers so are considered to be affected by the present global environment.

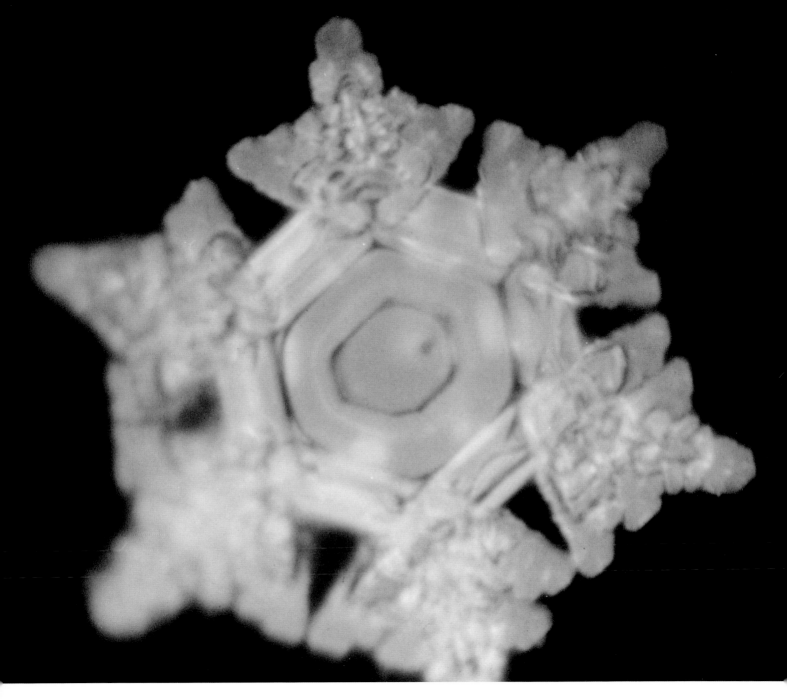

南極の氷

南極探検隊の隊員の一人が持ち帰ってくれた、推定37万年前の氷の結晶です。きれいに整って、結晶の見本のような写真です。ただその他の自然水と比較してもとくに際立って美しいということもないので、当時と比べて今の自然水が極端に汚染されているわけではないことがわかり、ちょっとホッとしています。

This is a crystal of ice that one of the Antarctic expedition members brought back. It is estimated to be 370,000 years old. This crystal is very organized and is a perfect model of crystal formation However, it is not as markedly beautiful as some other natural spring water crystals that we have seen. This means that today's natural water is not as contaminated as it was at one time in history. This is quite a relief.

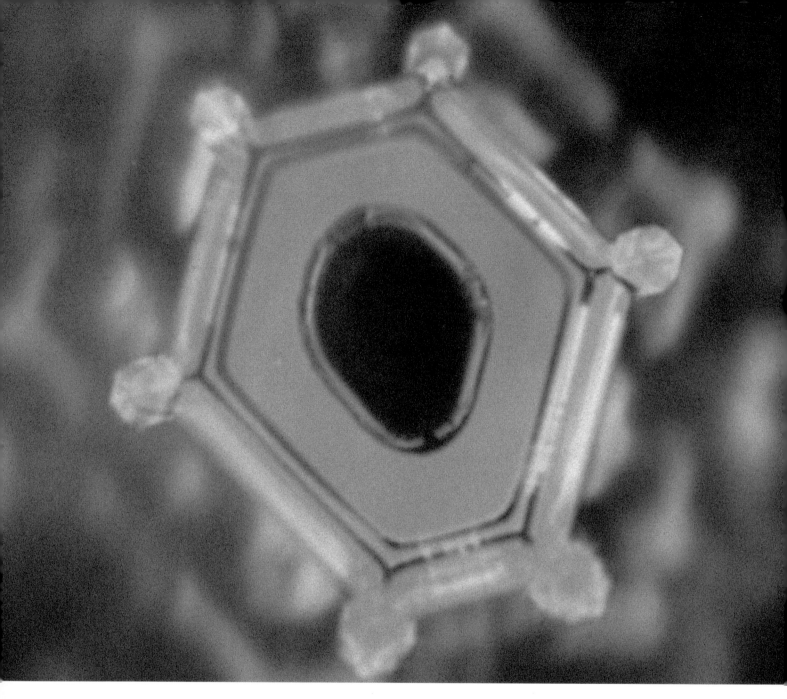

Columbia Glacier, Canada
カナダ・**コロンビア氷河**

カナディアン・ロッキー山脈には、いくつもの氷河があります。
万年雪となった氷から取り出された水の結晶は、しっかり六角形は保っているのですが、大きく空いた中心からは、どんな伝言を受け取ればいいのでしょう。

There are many glaciers in the Canadian Rocky Mountains.
This crystal of ice is extracted from firn, and maintains a firm hexagonal shape. What kind of message should be interpreted from the large void at the center of the crystal?

Mount Cook Glacier, New Zealand

ニュージーランド・マウントクック氷河

太平洋南西部、オーストラリアの南東部にある島国。北島と南島があって、北島の中央には活火山が連なり、南島には3,000メートルを超す山々が連なっています。その中に富士山とならぶ高さのマウントクックがあり、万年雪の氷河をもっています。その氷河の雪解け水の結晶写真です。

New Zealand is an island country located in the southwest Pacific Ocean, southeast of Australia.
It is composed of North Island and South Island. In North Island's central area there is an active volcano that is still in good shape.
On the South Island, there are mountains that exceed 3,000 meters. Among them is Mount Cook which is as high as Mount Fuji and has glacier of firn. This is the picture of a crystal taken from the melting water of that glacier.

地球上を循環する雨水

雨は天から降ってきます。

1年中、ほぼ同じ土地に、ほぼ同じ量だけ、降っています。

この自然の約束にしたがって、人は作物をつくり、水を飲み、水を汲み、山の木々もうるおっています。

そして地球上の水は、空に昇って雨になり、地上に降ってくることで、まるで天然自然の浄水器を通ったように、浄化されているのです。

結晶写真を撮影してわかったことは、当然のことながら、どんなに立派な浄水器よりも、自然の循環による浄化の方が素晴らしいということ。

湧き水や湖沼、河川などの真水のもとは、雨。

自然の湧き水からは美しい結晶が得られました。

今、地上に湧き出している湧き水は、おそらく何十、何百年以上も前に降った雨が、地中深く浸透する間に、多くの自然のろ過装置にあたる土や石の間をくぐり抜けてきたものです。そして水脈をつくり『ここぞ！』と思う位置に、また、『今だ！』という時期に湧き出ているのです。

そこで、湧き水のもとになる雨はどうでしょう。雨水を採取して結晶写真にしてみました。

環境破壊などの被害が指摘されています。人口の多い都市に降る雨と田舎に降る雨とでは、違うのでしょうか。

北と南、あるいは同じ土地でも季節によって違いはあるのでしょうか。

Rainwater

Rainwater that Circulates the Earth

Rain comes falling down from heaven.
All year round, the same amount of rain falls on the same land.
Because of this consistency, people can plan and grow crops, drink water, and pump water and trees in the mountains can have enough water.
The water of the earth becomes rain as it evaporates into the sky and then falls back to the ground. It is cleansed by passing through this natural water purification process.
What we learn from this crystal's picture is that of course, natural purification is much more effective than any mechanical water purifier, no matter how good.
Rain is the source of fresh water such as spring water, lakes, marshes and rivers.
We obtained this beautiful crystal from natural spring water.
The spring water that flows out onto the earth's surface passed through the natural filtering devices of soil and rocks when it fell as rain a few hundred years ago and penetrated into the ground.
The water then joins the spring water vein to flow out at a place that it feels is "the right place" and when it feels that it is "the right time".
What would the crystals look like for this rain which is the source of spring water?
We sampled rainwater and took a picture of the crystal.
Recently, there have been reports of damages due to environmental disruption. What is the water crystal difference between rain that falls on a densely populated urban area and rain that falls on a rural area?
Is there a difference between the rain that falls in the north or the south? Is there any difference between the rain that falls during different seasons at the same location?

Biei-cho, Hokkaido

北海道・美瑛町

北海道のほぼ中央、美瑛町は『北の国から』のロケ地のひとつです。
のどかな田園地帯に降る雨水は、悲しいかな……。北海道はとくにオゾン層破壊、酸性雨の被害が
大きいとされていることを立証してしまったようです。

Located in the center of Hokkaido, Biei-cho was chosen as one of the locations for "Kita-no-Kuni Kara, From the Northern Country."
The crystals from the rainwater that falls on this quiet rural region are saddening.
Hokkaido seems to have had obvious damage caused by ozone layer depletion and acid rain.

Sendai City, Miyagi Prefecture
宮城県・仙台市

仙台の雨水からは、きれいな結晶が得られたかと思えば、形にもならない時があるなど、時期によって大きなバラツキが出ました。原因ははっきりしませんが、雨水はその時の大気の状態などによって、大きく影響されるデリケートなもののようです。

The rainwater from the Sendai area sometimes showed beautiful crystals and sometimes showed those with an unshapely form. These were also great fluctuations in the crystals depending on the season.
This cause is not clear but rainwater seems to be very delicate and might have been affected by the condition of atmosphere at that time.

Kanazawa City, Ishikawa Prefecture
石川県・金沢市

古都金沢に降る雨からは、不思議な結晶が得られました。完全ではありませんが、六角形の結晶構造が見てとれます。
日本海側は太平洋側に比べて大きな工業地帯もなく、大気汚染の度合いが低いはずで、もう少し美しいものが撮れてもいいのに……と思ってしまいます。

From the rain that falls on the ancient city of Kanazawa, we obtained mysterious crystals. The crystal is not complete, but we can see a hexagonal crystal structure.
There aren't as many large industrial zones on the Japan Sea coast as there are on the Pacific Ocean coast, so it would follow that the air pollution level in this area would be lower. We feel that for this reason we should be able to obtain a beautiful water crystal from the Japan Sea coast than from the Pacific Ocean coast.

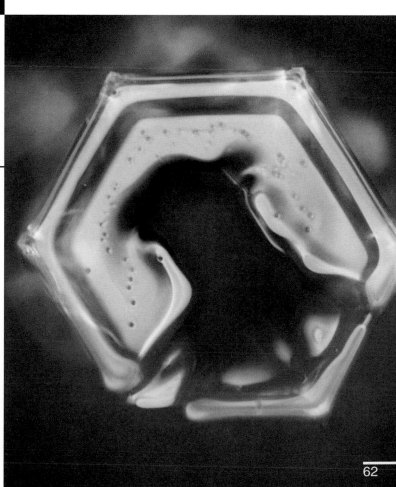

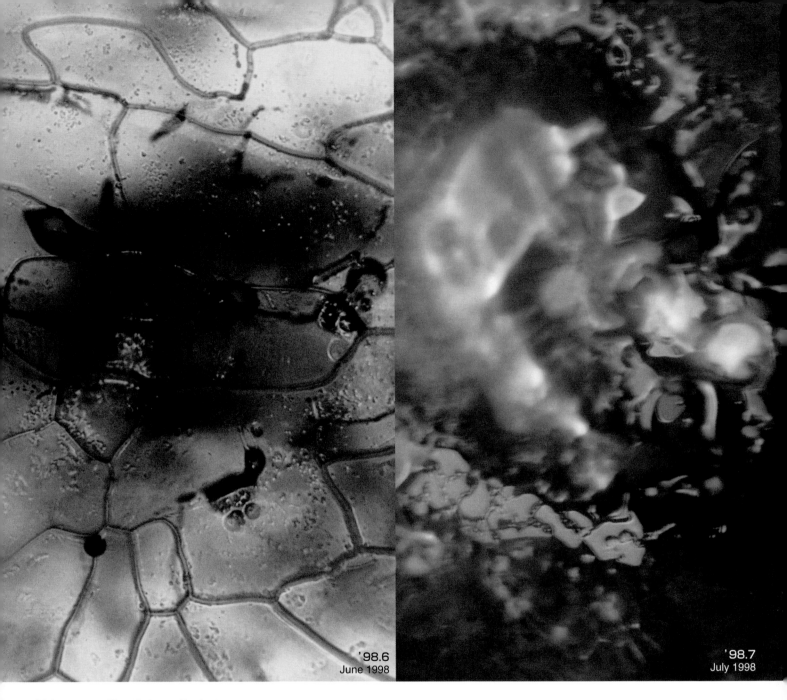

'98.6
June 1998

'98.7
July 1998

Tokorozawa City, Saitama Prefecture

埼玉県・所沢市

所沢の雨水を最初に撮影しはじめた（'98年6月）頃は、公開をはばかられるくらいにおぞましい映像でした。ところが右の写真のように最近になってくればくるほど、結晶がきれいになってきています。所沢市民の環境問題に対する関心が深まるにしたがって、美しい結晶になっていると判断せざるをえません。がんばれ所沢！

When we first started taking pictures of the rainwater in Tokorozawa City (June, 1998), the crystal's structure was so miserable that we hesitated to make it public. However, as you can see in the right picture, the crystal has become clearer recently. We cannot help but believe that as the citizens of Tokorozawa became aware of their city's environmental problems, it has started showing very beautiful crystals.
Stick to it, Tokorozawa!

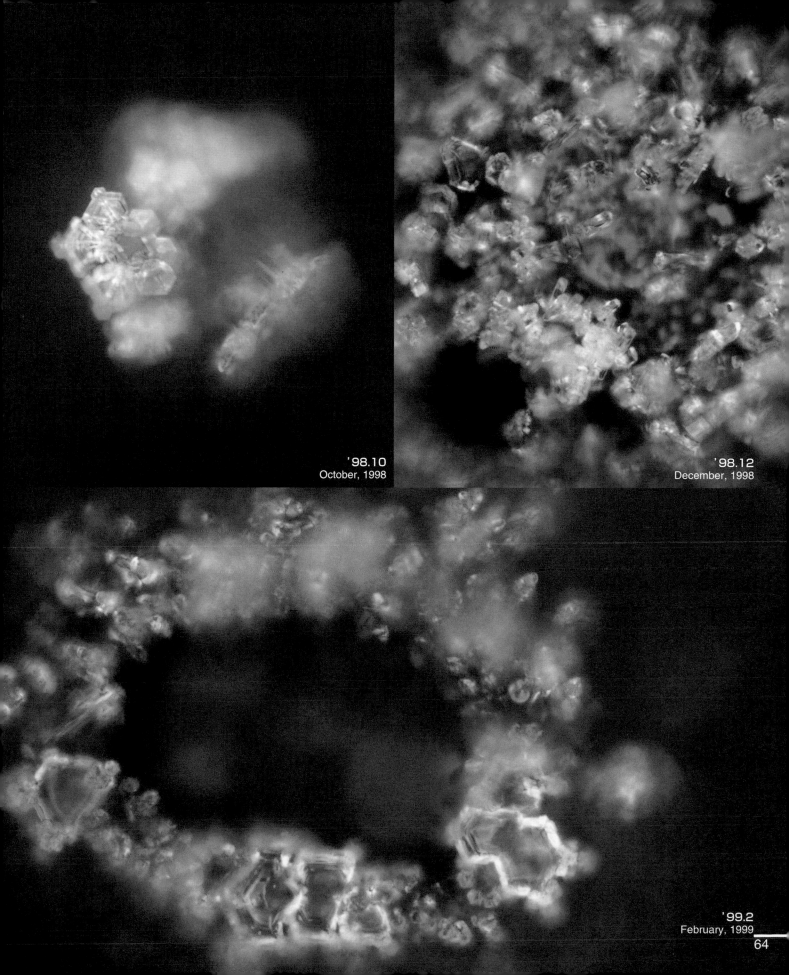

'98.10
October, 1998

'98.12
December, 1998

'99.2
February, 1999

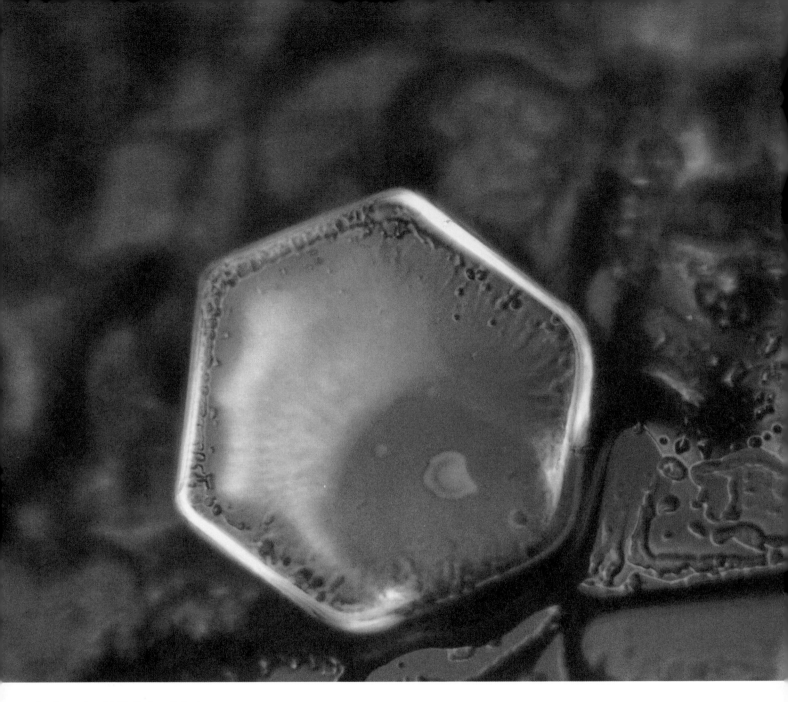

Asakusa-bashi, Taito-ku, Tokyo

東京都台東区・浅草橋

東京の真ん中にある浅草橋に降る雨でも、時には結晶を得られることがあります。
なかなか形の整ったきれいなものには出会えませんが、それでも水道水などと比べれば、自然の浄
化作用の素晴らしさを感じます。

We were able to get crystals from the rain that fell on the Asakusa-bashi at the center of Tokyo.
It was hard to find shapely and beautiful crystals from this water, but even so, we can see the effects of the natural purifying power of rain water. This is especially evident as compared with the crystals found in tap water.

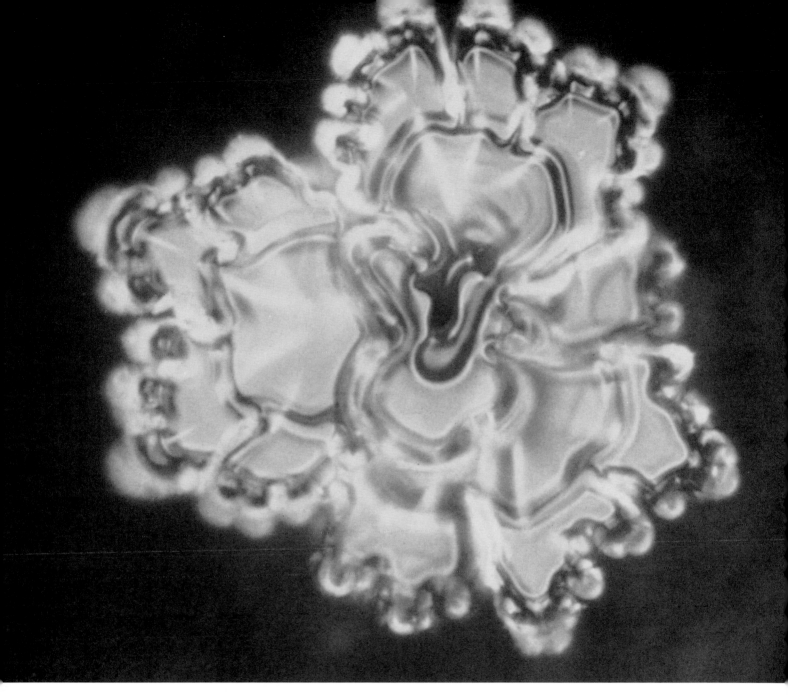

Fujisawa City, Kanagawa Prefecture

神奈川県・**藤沢市**

江の島を目の前に高級住宅地として歴史のある町。
ゆったりと、暮らしやすい土地柄で、風光明媚そのもの。しかし、この地の雨水は、まるで酸性雨
によって六角形が溶けてメロメロになってしまったような気がしてしまいますが……。

Fujisawa is a historic city in front of Enoshima and a prestigious residential area.
The city has beautiful scenery, is comfortable and easy to live in. However because of acid rain, the rainwater
crystal from this area melted away leaving no trace of a hexagonal shape.

Okazaki City, Aichi Prefecture
愛知県・岡崎市

名古屋市の隣り、岡崎市でも整った結晶を見ることはできませんでした。ある時期には結晶化しそうなものも見られるのですが、それを妨げる要因の方が強いようです。
これらの写真からは「混沌」としたイメージや、水自身のもどかしさが感じられます。

We could not see an organized shape in the crystal taken from the rainwater in Okazaki City where is adjacent to Nagoya City. At one point we could see crystals that were close to formulating, but the factors that impeded their formation seemed to be stronger.
While looking at these crystals we felt the sense of chaos in the images. It is as if the water itself is irritated.

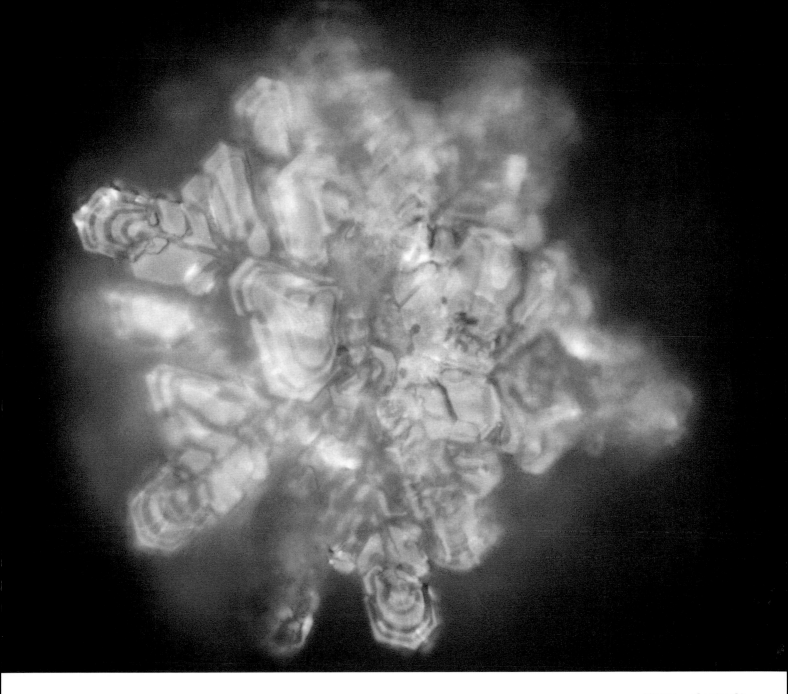

Nishi-ku, Osaka City
大阪市・西区

大阪市内のオフィス街で採取した雨水の中で、あえて一番きれいに撮れたものをご紹介しました。やはり結晶に歪みはあります。きれいな結晶にはなっていませんが、結晶化しようとする意志は見えるようです。

From the rainwater that was sampled from the office quarters of Osaka City we find the most beautiful picture of a crystal.
There is a distortion in the crystal and it has not become fully developed but we can see its will to become crystallized.

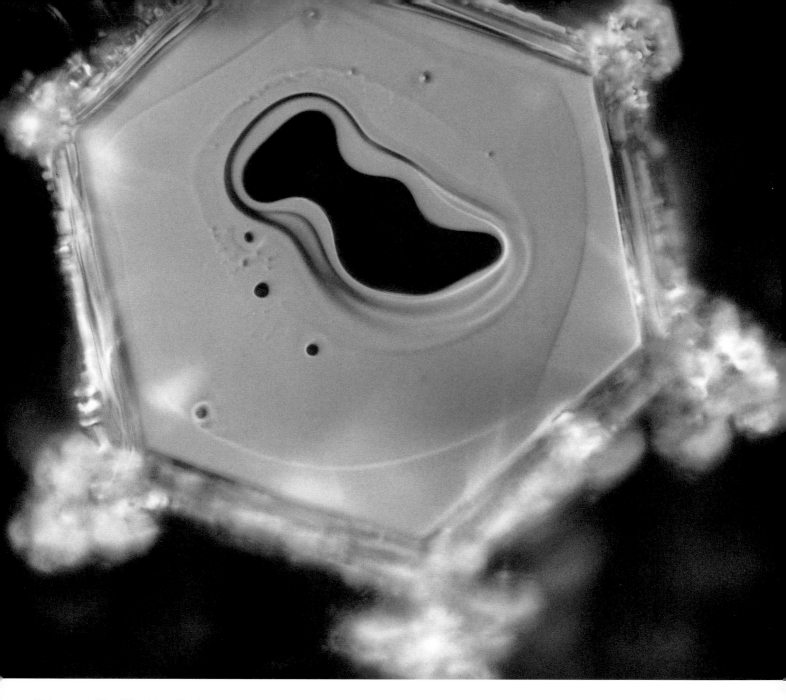

Fukuyama City, Hiroshima Prefecture
広島県・福山市

瀬戸内海の海岸にある福山市は、空襲を受けたために戦後大開発をされた町です。
六角構造の名残りは確認できるものの、どれも歪んでいたり、亀裂が入っていたり。しかし、これらの写真からは、なんとなく「頑張っている」感じが伝わってきて、応援したくなるような結晶です。

Fukuyama City is located on the coast of the Seto Inland Sea. It was re-developed after the world war because it was destroyed by bombing.
We can identify remnants of a hexagonal structure, but most of the crystal structure is either distorted or cracked. From these pictures however, we can feel that it is "trying hard" to develop and we want to support its efforts.

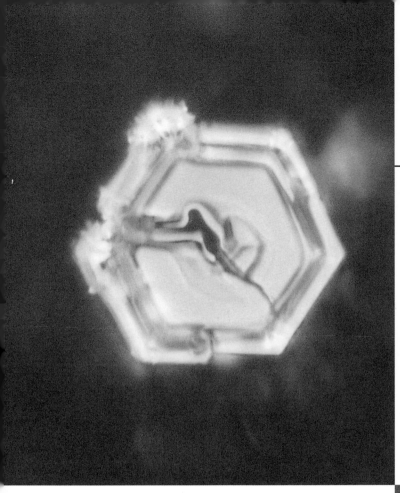

福岡市・博多区

九州一の大都市・博多の雨水も、酸性雨の被害は免れられないようです。
結晶の形は少し歪んでいますが、六角形が見えるものもあれば、整った結晶が無残にも真っ二つに割れてしまったものも……。
水は市民に何を訴えているのでしょうか。

A crystal taken from a sample of the rain in Hakata, the largest city in Kyushu. Alas, this crystal could not seem to evade the damage done from acid rain.
The crystal shape is slightly distorted, but seems to be a hexagon and some of the clearer crystals have split in two. What is the water crystal trying to ask its city's citizens?

Kagoshima City, Kagoshima Prefecture

鹿児島県・鹿児島市

六角構造に枝が伸びている、不思議な姿のきれいな結晶が得られました。ほかの都市と比べても、希望がもてます。
桜島の火山灰は雨水の結晶にどのような影響があるのか、などと思います。

In this picture, we obtained the shape of a mystical figure imbedded in a clear crystal with branches stretching out from the hexagonal structure. As compared with the crystals from other cities, there is hope in this one.
We could not help but wonder what affect the volcanic ashes of Sakurajima have on the surrounding rainwater?

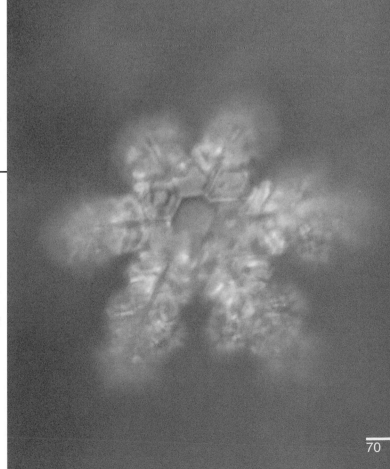

第二章　変化する水の話

水が音を聴いているの!?

最近、百貨店の店頭などで『このピロシキは生地を発酵させる際、チャイコフスキーの名曲を聞かせて、美味しくまろやかに仕上げた音楽食品です』などという宣伝文句が掲げられ、行列ができています。また、もっとも科学的な分野といわれる医療の現場でも、最近、音楽療法の技術が取り入れられはじめています。

植物に意識があるという説もなかば公認されつつあります。植物を育てるとき「元気に育ってね」とやさしく声をかけてあげるのと、「枯れてしまえ」などと嫌な言葉をかけるのとでは、生育状態に歴然とした差が出るそうです。

ここで考えました。

食物や植物の中に含まれている水が音楽や言葉を聴いているのではないかと。人が音楽を聴いて楽しくなったり、元気づけられたりするということは、人の身体の中の水が変化したためではないかと考えたのです。

空気中を伝わってきた音楽や言葉の振動が、もっとも影響を与えるのは水なのではないでしょうか。

『音楽や言葉の振動が、植物や食品の水に影響を与えている』。さらに『良い音楽や良い言葉が、それらの水に良い影響を与えている』らしいと思いました。

これを何らかの形で実証することはできないか。音楽や言葉が水に与える影響を表現する方法としても、結晶写真は素晴らしく有効です。

Chapter 2　A Story of Ever-changing Water

Water Listens to Sound?

Recently, we see advertisements such as "Our piroshki is now a 'musical food'." We tried to enhance its naturally mellow flavor by playing music composed by Tchaikovsky while it was fermenting." Out of curiosity, people lined up to buy this product. Also recently, music therapy technology is being introduced in medical institutions, which is said to be the most scientific field.

Additionally, theories saying that plants also have consciousness are becoming more public. When we grow plants by saying sweet things to them such as "Please grow up healthy" or alternately by saying mean things such as, "Go on and get withered", these theories say that the plants show a clear difference in their growing progressions.

These theories made us think.

The water contained in food and plants must be listening to music and words.

People can become joyous and encouraged when they listen to music, all because the water contained in their bodies goes through a change.

The vibrations of music and words transmitted through the air effects water more than any other element.

"The vibrations of music and words affect the water that is contained in plants and food." Furthermore, "good music and kind words must exert a positive effect on water."

Is there any way to demonstrate this theory? Pictures of crystals are wonderfully effective as a method to view the effect that music and words exert on water.

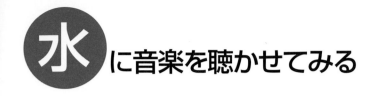水 に音楽を聴かせてみる

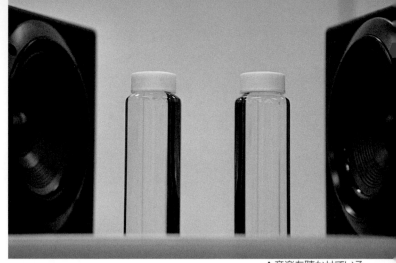

▲音楽を聴かせている
Playing music to water

どうやって水に音楽を?!

ベースになる「基本の水」には、不純物がもっとも少なく、シンプルな結晶構造を持つ精製水を採用。ところが年を追って精製水そのものが、良い結晶をもたなくなってきました。お見せするのは、一部の良いものです。

まず基本の精製水の結晶写真をカメラに収め、その水に右上の写真の状態で音楽を聴かせた後、結晶にし撮影したものです。

「どのように音楽を聴かせるのがもっとも良いのか」「ジャンルは？　時間は？　音量は？　スピーカーとの距離は？」などなど。じつに細々とした実験方法が、さらに私たちを悩ませました。試行錯誤の結果、

★2つのスピーカーの中間に精製水を置いて、通常程度の音量で、1曲完全に聴かせる

★精製水のビンの底を必ずよく叩き、一晩、置く

★翌日さらによく叩き、その水を凍らせて結晶を撮影……という手順を確立しました。

これがベストの方法かどうかはわかりませんが、現時点でのベターな方法と思われます。とくに「よく叩く」ということが結構重要で、これを怠ると結晶の出現率が低下するのです。振動を与えることによって、水に伝わってきた情報が活性化するらしいのです。とにかく、そうした苦労の末に、撮影された結晶写真です。

また、結晶は2つと同じものがないということから、確かに撮影するたびに違った結晶ができます。ですから次ページは、100のサンプルの中からランダムに取り出したものです。類似性を確認してみてください。

音楽の次は『水に文字を見せる』ことを考えつきました。無謀を覚悟でチャレンジです。さらに人の意識で、どこまで水が変化するのかという実験にも挑戦しました。

前人未到のジャングルを行く気分です。

Playing Music to Water

How Do We Play Music to Water?

We selected distilled water as the base water to do our experiments on because it has a simple crystal structure with the least number of impurities. We did find that some distilled water tends to lose the ability to form well-structured crystals as recentiy. What you see here are only those samples that started out having well formed crystals. First, we took pictures of basic distilled water then after playing music (under the conditions shown in the upper right picture) we crystallized them and took their picture again. "What is the best way to play music so that we get the optimum effects on the crystals?" "What should the genre of the music be? For how long? What is the volume? How long should the distance from the speaker to the crystals be?" We had to spend a lot of time planning our detailed experimentation methods. As a result of trial and error, we decided on the following procedures:
Place the distilled water in between 2 speakers and play one piece of musicfully at a normal volume. Tap the bottom of the distilled water bottle and leave overnight. Tap well again the next day before freezing the water to make crystals. Take pictures of the crystals.
We do not know if this is the best method or not, but we feel that it is the best method that we know at this present point in time. In particular, tapping the container well is a rather important component because when we neglected to do it the crystallization rate declined. By applying this tapping vibration, information seemed to be transmitted through the water causing the crystals to activate. Anyway, these are the pictures of the crystals that were seen as a result of such strenuous efforts. Because there is no crystal that is identical to another, we obtained different crystal forms each time we took a picture. The next page, confirms the similarities that can be found among pictures taken of 100 random samples. Following our music experiments, we decided to see how water responds to words. We also challenged ourselves to conduct experiments to see how much water is effected by human consciousness. It felt like we were setting foot in a jungle that no one has ever explored before.

Similarity of Crystal Pictures

結晶写真の類似性

Pictures of the 100 Samples are Similar...

100のサンプルから撮影して得られる結晶写真は、よく似て……

▲ '94年11月頃、撮影した精製水　Distrilled water photographed in around November 1994

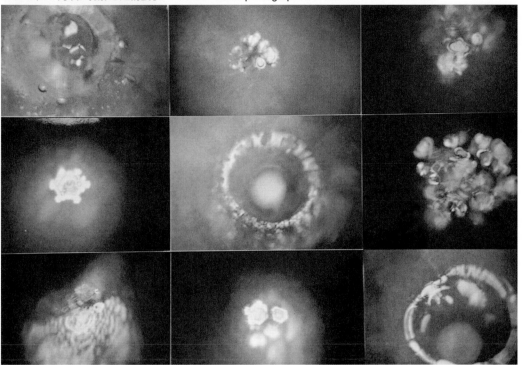

73ページ、右上の写真のようにセッティングし、音楽を聴かせて撮影した写真は、これまた見事な姿を見せてくれました。

基本の精製水・100のサンプルの結晶をそれぞれ撮影し、ランダムに選び出したものです。

A sample of water that we placed as shown in upper right picture on page 73 and then exposed to music showed some wonderful shapes.
The left hand pictures are of the crystals from 100 basic distilled water to select them at random.

▲ '96年3月頃の精製水の結晶写真
Crystal pictures of distilled water in around March 1996

▼ '96年3月頃に精製水に波動ミュージックを聴かせて撮影した結晶写真
Crystal pictures of distilled water after playing Hado music around March 1996

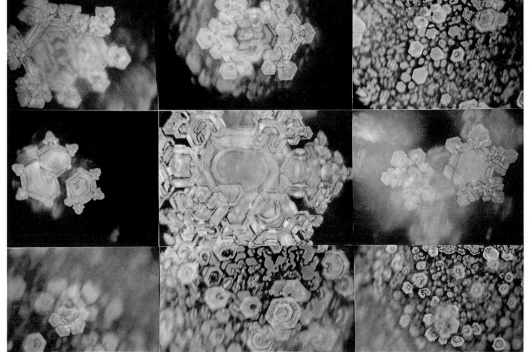

左の写真は、上の基本の精製水に音楽、それも身体に心地よいヒーリングミュージック「Hado」CDを聴かせた水の結晶のいろいろ。

ひとつひとつのシャーレによって、結晶の形は違いますが、ご覧のように類似性は認められると思います。

In the left hand pictures are crystals of water that have been exposed with a playing of a healing music called "Hado". This music is known for its ability to relax the body. In each container the shape of the crystals differed, but as you can see, we think that there are also some similarities.

Beethoven's "Pastorale"

ベートーベン「田園」

ベートーベンの作品を代表する交響曲のひとつで、明るく爽やかで楽しい曲です。
良い曲は水を活性化させ、成長を促進させることを裏付けるような美しい結晶です。

This is one of Beethoven's most famous symphonies and is a bright, fresh and joyous piece.
This beautiful crystal supports the fact that good music positively effects water.

Mozart's "Symphony No. 40 in G Minor"

モーツァルト 「交響曲第40番ト短調」

モーツァルト全交響曲のなかでも、つねに美しいものを追及する魂の唄……美への祈りとも思える深い思いが込められた曲。聴く人の心を静かに癒してくれます。
結晶は作曲者の気持ちを代弁するように、美しく、たおやかにできあがっています。

This symphony is a soulful song that seems to pursue beauty the most of any of the works of Mozart. A piece of deep thought that seems almost like a prayer to beauty. This music quietly heals the heart of its listeners.
This crystal is so beautiful and graceful that it's as if it's speaking on behalf of the composer's feelings.

Bach's "Air for the G String"
バッハ「G線上のアリア」

有名なヴァイオリン曲。ヴァイオリンの音色にうっとりして誘われるかのように、水の結晶も枝の部分が大きく伸びやかに成長しています。
結晶がなんとなく、楽しげに踊っているような印象さえ受ける写真です。

Through this famous violin piece, the crystal seems as if it has been enchanted by the sound of the music. The branches of the water crystal stretch out freely.
This picture gives the impression that the crystal is dancing merrily.

Bach's "Goldberg Variations"

バッハ「ゴールトベルク変奏曲」

この曲は、バッハがお世話になった伯爵のためにつくった就寝曲（子守歌？）を、ゴールトベルク
という男性に弾かせたものとか……。基本の精製水と比べると、六角形の角からさらに別の六角形
が成長している様子がはっきりとわかります。感謝の気持ちが結晶の成長を促進しています。

"Bach's Goldberg Variations, which explores a vast emotional palette, is one of the greatest monuments of the keyboard repertoire."
As compared with crystals that grow from pure distilled water, here you can see that one hexagon is growing from the edge of another.
It is worth thinking about the feelings of thankfulness that are written into this set of variations and their ability to promote positive spiritual growth.

Chopin's "Farewell Song"
ショパン「別れの曲」

ピアノ曲として有名で、メロディーを聴けば誰でも知っているお馴染みの曲です。
そしてこの結晶を得たときほどびっくりしたことはありませんでした。「別れの曲」だからでしょうか、基本の結晶の形が見事に細分化され、まさしく「別れ別れ」になってしまいました。顕微鏡の倍率は同じなのに……です。

This is such a famous piano music piece that almost anyone can recall this music once they hear it.
I have never been so astonished as I was when I obtained this crystal. Is it shaped the way that it is because it is effected by "Farewell Song"? The basic crystal shape is almost perfectly divided into small parts that have become "separated" from each other. This, despite the fact that the magnifying power of the microscope, is the same as it was in the other photos.

ヒーリングミュージック「Hado」
Healing Music, "Hado"

これは痛みをやわらげ、身体の免疫力を高めることを目的に、特別な技術を駆使してアメリカでつくられたヒーリングミュージックのCDを聴かせたものです。枝の部分がニョキニョキと力強く伸びており、まるで栄養価の高いキノコのような美しい結晶写真になりました。
実際にこの曲を聴いて、いろいろな生理的効果があったことが、多数報告されています。

This is a picture of a crystal of water that has been exposed to a CD (Composed by Alan Roubik) of healing music that was created in the USA. This music is said to make use of a special technology with the purpose of easing pain and enhancing physical immunity. The branch section of the crystal stretches out and becomes elongated. The resulting picture is beautiful, resembling a highly nutritious mushroom. We have received many reports from users that also felt various physiological effects by listening to this piece.

Tibet Sutra
チベットのお経

映画「セブン・イヤーズ・イン・チベット」の中でも流された、お経のCDを聞かせたもの。
力強く、美しい結晶が撮れました。古くから伝えられているお経は、人々の魂に語りかけ、それを
癒す強いエネルギーを持っているであろうことが確認できます。

This is a picture of crystal of water that formed after being exposed to a CD of the music from the sound track of the movie, "Seven Years in Tibet."
We were able to take a picture of a powerful and beautiful crystal. We can reaffirm the ancient knowledge that the Sutra talks to people's souls and has a strong positive energy that can heal people's feelings.

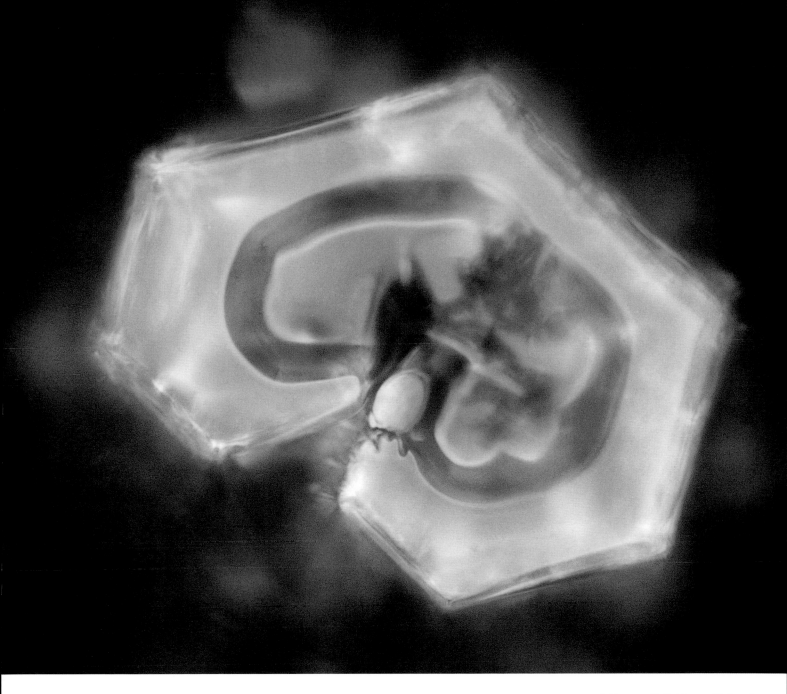

A Korean Folk Song, "Ariran"

韓国民謡「アリラン」

ご存じ、朝鮮の民謡。アリラン峠を越えて別れていく、恋人同士の別離の歌。
旅立つ男性を、残る女性が見送る……菅原都々子さんの歌を聴かせました。
なにか、つらく、切ない、胸の痛くなるような結晶ではありませんか。

This is a famous Korean folk song about two lovers who are forced to be separated as they cross the Arian mountain pass.
The girl sends off her departing lover with a song sung by Sugawara Tsuzuko.
Doesn't this crystal have a somewhat painful, sad and heartbreaking look?

Kawachi Folk Dance Song

「河内音頭」

河内地方で800年も伝承されている音頭。
現在活躍中の河内家菊水丸さんの提案で、彼の歌う河内音頭を聴かせた水の結晶です。
長い間、多くの人々によって歌い継がれている曲には、人を癒す力があるのではないでしょうか。

A folk dance song handed down in the Kawachi region for more than 800 years.
This is a crystal of water that we exposed to Kawachi Folk Dance Song. This idea was suggested by Mr. Kawachiya Kikusuimaru and was sung by himself.
For hundreds of years this music has been cherished and sung by many people and because of this it may have some healing power.

「川の流れのように」
Just Like a Flowing River

クラシックやヒーリングミュージックと比べて歌謡曲はどうでしょう。
昭和を代表する歌手、美空ひばりさんの「川の流れのように」。時を越えて歌い継がれる良い曲は、
やはり良い気・波動をもっています。聴く人の心をほっとさせるような、均整のとれた美しい結晶
です。でも、ぽっかりと空いた空洞は何を物語るのでしょうか。

How about trying popular music as compared with classical music and healing music? "Just Like a Flowing
River" was sung by Misora Hibari, a famous singer of the Showa Era. When this timeless and wonderful piece
is sung, there can be no doubts as to its positive energy and HADO. The crystal that formed is well balanced in
a way that reflects the nostalgic feelings of the listeners.
But what is the meaning of the gaping hole?

Folk Song of Celtic Region, UK

イギリス・ケルト地方の民謡から

日本でもお馴染みの歌手エンヤさんの曲は、『ガイア・シンフォニー第一番』にも使われていて、
リラクゼーションなどのヒーリング効果があるとか。
どの曲も不思議な、独特の世界をもっています。
この写真はそれを証明するかのように、優しく繊細で美しい結晶をみせてくれました。

This music is sung by Enya who is well-known in Japan and elsewhere. We used the piece, "Gaia Symphony No.1," which is said to have the healing effects of relaxation. Each piece of her music has its own mystical unique world.
 This picture shows a tender and delicately beautiful crystal.

Elvis Presley's "Heartbreak Hotel"

エルビス・プレスリー
「HEARTBREAK HOTEL」

エルビス・プレスリーさんの「HEARTBREAK HOTEL」を聴かせたところ、3種類の結晶が撮れました。
上の写真は、まさしくハートが2つにわかれてしまったハートブレイクな写真。
右の写真は、それが融合しようとしている写真。
下の写真は、試練に絶えて、新たなハートの形成をしていると考えるのは、ちょっとセンチに過ぎるでしょうか？

Heartbreak Hotel by Elvis Presley
When we exposed the water to "Heartbreak Hotel" sung by Elvis Presley, we were able to obtain three types of crystals.
The picture, above, is a picture of a heart broken into two.
The picture, right, shows the two parts trying to fuse together.
The picture, below, shows a newly formed heart that overcame the difficult period. Do you think that this idea is too sentimental?

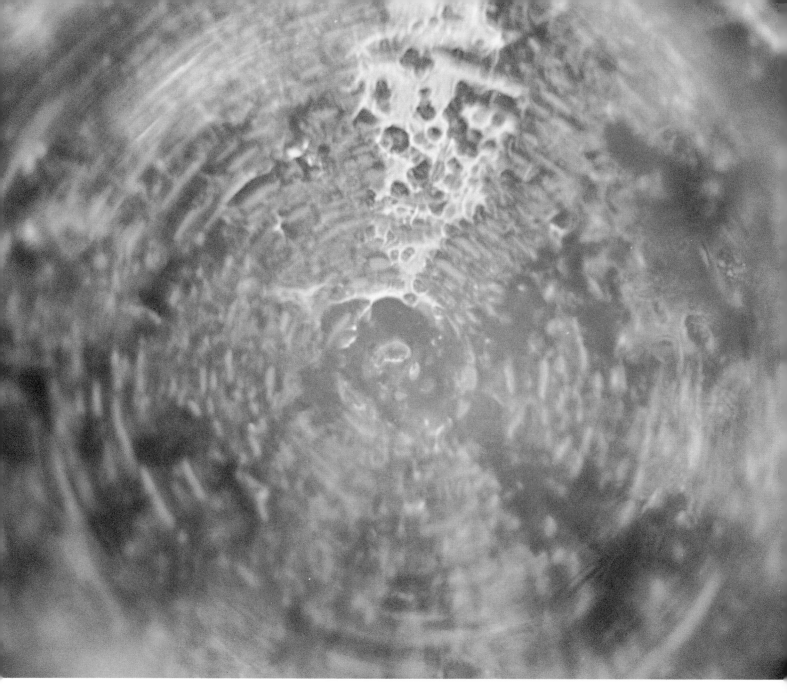

A Heavy Metal Music
あるヘヴィーメタルの曲

歌詞の内容は怒りがいっぱい。世の中を罵倒しているような曲です。基本の整った六角形の結晶構造が、見事にバラバラに壊れてしまっています。この曲に対して水は、はっきりとネガティブな反応を示したようです。ただしヘヴィーメタルが悪いというわけではなく、歌詞に問題があったと考えられますが、あくまでも一つの例です。

This music is filled with anger and seems to be denouncing the world. Subsequently, this crystal's basic well-formed hexagonal structure has broken into perfect pieces. The water seems to have reacted negatively to this music. We are not saying that heavy metal music is bad, only that there must have been a problem with the lyrics. This is merely an example.

日本のあるヒット曲

若者に絶大な人気を誇るグループの曲で、ヒットチャートではいつも上位にありました。
しかし結晶になると、六角構造が崩れてしまい、四角い無味乾燥の結晶になっています。
ヒット曲が必ずしも良い結晶になる、というわけではない例としてご紹介します。

This is a song that is sung by a group who is very popular in Japan, and it is always at the top of the hit chart. However, when we look at the crystal, we can see its broken hexagonal structure and it's subsequent square unattractive shape.

We are introducing this example only to show that hit music does not always contribute to the production of well-formed crystals.

ごはんに毎日『ありがとう！』『ばかやろう！』と声をかけた！

　講演の席で、水に文字を見せる（90ページ参照）実験内容を発表しました。するとそれに呼応しておもしろい実験をしてくれた方がいます。

　その実験とは、「普通に炊いたお米を2つの同じガラス容器に入れ、一方には『ありがとう』、もう一方には『ばかやろう』と言葉に出して毎日声をかけ、それを1ヵ月間観察する」というものでした。

　小学生の子どもが2人、学校から帰ると毎日、ランドセルを放り出しては、瓶に貼った文字のとおりに声をかけるという日課を1ヵ月続けました。そしてその結果、『ありがとう』と声をかけ続けたごはんは、半ば発酵状態となり、匂いを嗅ぐと芳醇な麹のような良い香りに。一方『ばかやろう』のごはんは真っ黒に変色して腐り、その臭いたるや……ひどいものでした。

　もちろんこれはキチンとした研究機関が行った実験ではありませんから、たまたまそうなったと言われれば、それまでですが。その後、同じような実験をやってくれた人が何人も現われて、同じ結果となっています。

　ここでは「水」だけでなく、微生物さんが深く関わっているようです。微生物さんも、われわれと同じで、ほめられれば良く働くし、けなされればふて寝をしてしまうのでしょう。

　『ありがとう』『ばかやろう』と声をかけ続けたことで微生物は善玉菌と悪玉菌に分かれてしまったのではないかと思われます。

Speaking "Thank you" and "You fool" to Rice Everyday

While presenting a speech on the experiment that we did with the effects of language on water (see page 90), one of the audience members told me that they were very impressed. At that time, this person also told me about an interesting experiment. This experiment involved placing cooked rice in two identical glass containers. Afterwards he/she talked to the rice everyday saying "Thank you" to one and "You fool" to the other. He/She did this for one month to see the results. Two elementary school children talked to the rice everyday for one month as soon as they came home from school. As a result, the rice that the children had said "Thank you" to, was nearly fermented and had a nice mellow malted rice aroma. The other bowl of rice that the children had said "You fool" to, had turned black and had rotted.
They said that its smell was disgusting beyond description.
Of course this is not an experiment that an official research institute did, so the result could have been just a coincidence. However, many people have done the same experiment and they showed the same results. Here, not only water but microbes seem to be involved. Microbes are just like us, they work hard if they are praised and become idle if they are abused.
It seems that by saying "Thank you" and "You fool", the microbes must have grouped into beneficial bacteria and disadvantageous bacteria.

水に文字を見せる

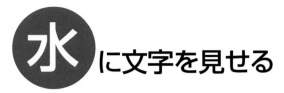

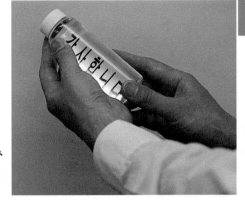

水が文字によって変化する？

水に音楽を聴かせるという私たちの試みに対して、水は想像以上の変化を見せてくれました。

そこで次に「言葉に対して水はどういう変化を見せるのか？」と考えました。ところが、言葉には響きがあります。たとえば『ばか！』と怒鳴るのと、『ばかねぇ～』と優しく言うのとでは違うのではないかと思いました。

それならということで「水に言葉（＝文字）を見せる」という方法を考えました。それも、人の手書き文字ではなく、ワープロで打った一定の文字を瓶に貼りました。あとから考えても「水に文字を見せる」なんて、世間一般の常識からは、はずれた発想だったかもしれません。が、撮影実験班は実行あるのみです。

ベースになる水は、音楽の時と同じ『基本の精製水』を使用。この水を2つに分けてガラス瓶に入れました。一方に「ありがとう」、もう一方には「ばかやろう」という文字をワープロで打った紙を貼りつけて、一晩放置。これを凍らせて写真撮影しました。

ところが水は言葉、文字によって、明らかな違いをみせてくれました。実験者には何も知らせず実験したり、実験者を変えてみても、同じような傾向が得られました。

Showing Letters to Water

Does Water Change after Showing Words to Water?

The water crystals showed various reactions to our attempts to expose them to music. So much so that we could not even have imagined the effects. Our next question lead us to ask, what kind of reaction does water show to words or to the sounds that words make? For instance, there is a great difference between angrily yelling "You fool!" and saying "You are a fool" in a gentle way.

So we decided to use language with our water samples. In other words, to "speak" to our water. We decided not to use handwritten words but rather words that were typed by a word processor. Looking back, our idea of speaking to water may have deviated from general common sense, but the photography team simply went on with the idea.

For the base water on which to experiment, we used basic distilled water. This was the same water that we used for experimenting with music.

We divided this water sample into two parts and placed them into glass bottles. We then pasted a paper on one bottle that had "Thank you" typed on it. On the other bottle we put "You fool". We then left them both that way for one night. The next day we froze this water and took pictures of the crystals that formed.

What we found was that the two water samples showed conspicuous differences from each other. We did the experiments without giving any information to the experimenting team. We also changed the experiment staff and ran the tests again, but we obtained the same results both times.

ありがとう
Thank You in Japanese

Thank You in Hangul

Thank you

Thank You
ありがとう

基本の精製水は「ばかやろう」と同じ水です。とても美しく均整のとれた形です。78ページの「ゴールドベルク変奏曲」を聞かせた結晶と見比べると、なんとなく形が似ています。
「ゴールドベルク変奏曲」はバッハが感謝の意を表わすためにつくった曲でした。日本語のありがとうの語源は、有り難く存在している……というような意味をもっています。
韓国語も英語もまた違った語源からきているのでしょう。

In this experiment we used basic distilled water and the words "Thank you" in the same way as we did in the "You fool" experiment. The crystal has a very beautiful, well-balanced shape.
It has a similar shape as the crystal that was exposed to "Goldberg Variations" on page 78. "Goldberg Variations" was composed by Bach to express his gratitude. The word, "Thank you" in Japanese exists to help us express gratitude. Korean and English must have derived differently.

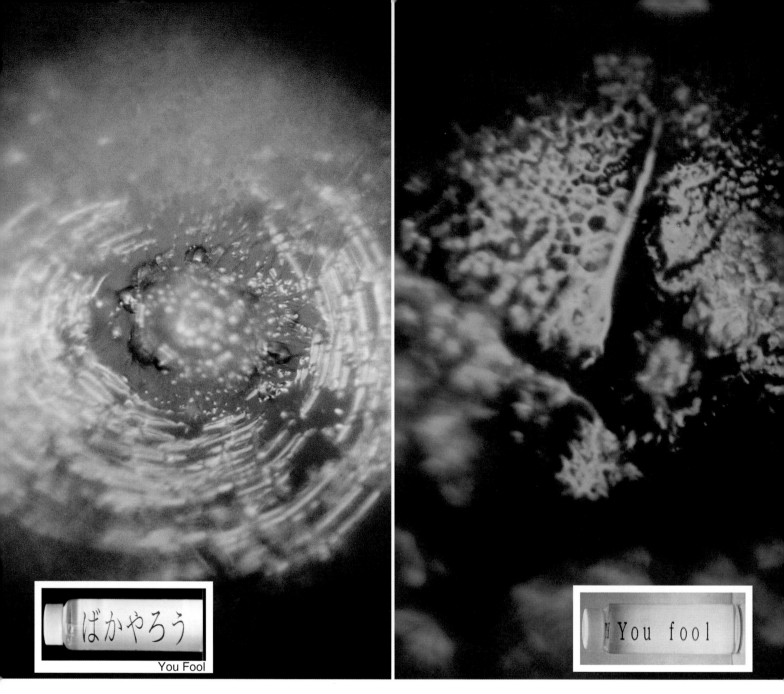

ばかやろう
You Fool

You Fool

ばかやろう

一晩中、瓶に貼りつけられた『ばかやろう』という文字を見ていた水です。87ページにあるヘヴィーメタルの曲を聴かせた水の写真とたいへん似通っています。その曲は社会に対して『ばかやろう』と叫んでいるような歌詞でしたから、そうなるのかもしれません……。また同じ意味をもつ、英語の『You Fool』も貼ってみました。言葉の持つ語源によっても差がでてくるようです。

This is the water that had the word "You fool" on its bottle overnight. This is crystal is similar to the one from the water that was exposed to heavy metal music on page 87. The lyrics from the music were similar to saying "you fool" to society, so the consequence may have been the same. We also pasted the words, "You fool" in English to another bottle. It seems that there is difference in the etymology of words because we did not obtain the same results.

ムカツク・殺す

You Make Me Sick. I Will Kill You

You Make Me Sick. I Will Kill You
ムカツク・殺す

最近、若者がよく口にする言葉ですが、予想通り水の姿は醜悪なものでした。
結晶が醜く歪み、潰れ、飛び散っている様子は、まさしく「ムカツク・殺す」そのもの。
こういう言葉が横行する世の中は不気味です。なんとか……みんなの手で！

These are words that young people often use these days. Subsequently the shape of the water was as ugly as we had expected after we exposed the sample to these words. The crystal was distorted, imploded and dispersed. It really was a visual image of the words, "you make me sick" and "I will kill you." That we exist in a world where words like this are used rampantly is awe inspiring. We have to do something ourselves.

Love/Appreciation

愛・感謝

愛と感謝に含まれる人の意識

　数多くの結晶写真を撮影してきましたが、当時ではこれ
ほど美しい結晶は見たことがありませんでした。

　やはり、この世の中で「愛と感謝」の気持ちに勝るもの
はないということ。

　「愛と感謝」を表現するだけで、身の回りの水、また身
体の中の水がこんなに美しく変化してくれるのだったら…
…。

　なんとか、日常の生活に生かせるといいですね。

　また92ページの「Thank you」の結晶ともよく似ている
のがうれしくなってしまいます。

People's consciousness contained in love and appreciation. We took pictures of numerous crystals from this sample but this was the very first beautiful crystal that we saw.

Indeed, there is nothing more important than love and gratitude in this world. Just by expressing love and gratitude, the water around us and in our bodies changes so beautifully. We want to apply this in our daily lives, don't we?

Strong resemblance to the crystal with the words, "Thank you" on page 92 was a happy coincidence.

愛　感謝

Love/Appreciation

96

魂
Soul

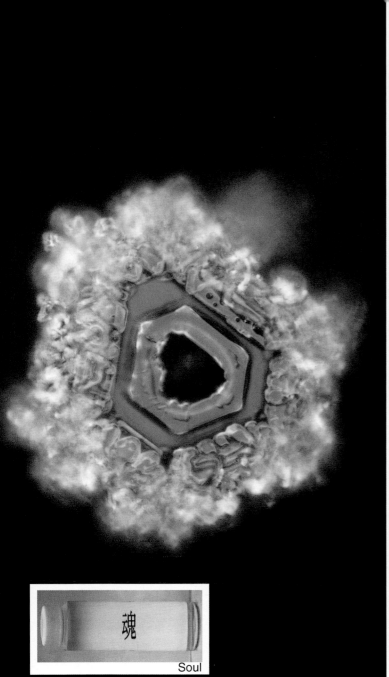

魂

Soul

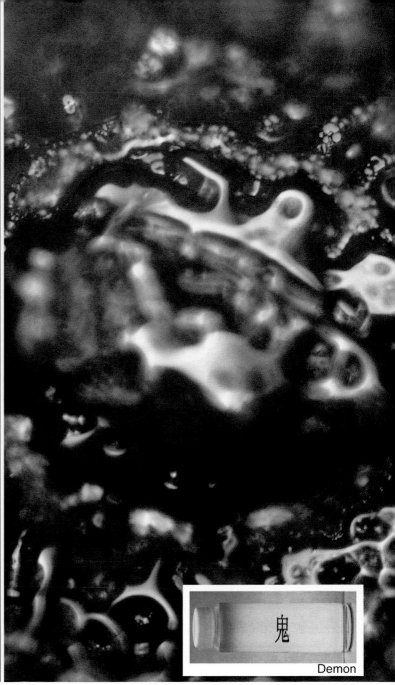

鬼

Demon

Soul/Demon

魂・鬼

魂という文字の「云」の部分を取ると鬼という字になります。人は言いたいことを言わないと鬼になってしまうということでしょうか。水は魂を認識し、形にして、われわれ人間に伝言してきました……。2枚の写真から、どんな印象を受け取ればいいのでしょう。中心にハート型が見えると思うのは、考えすぎでしょうか。そして鬼は……。

We have the letter, soul by removing the left part of the letter (which means "telling"), demon. People become demons if they do not express their opinions. In this picture, the water crystal recognizes the word soul and give us humans this message. What kind of impression should we make from the two pictures? Is it exaggerating to see a heart shape in the center?

天使

Angel

天使

Angel

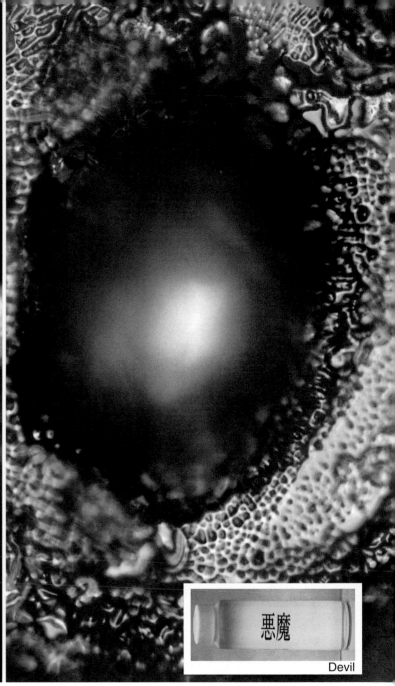

悪魔

Devil

Angel/Devil
天使と悪魔

いかがでしょうか……。

What do you think?

しょうね

Let's Do It

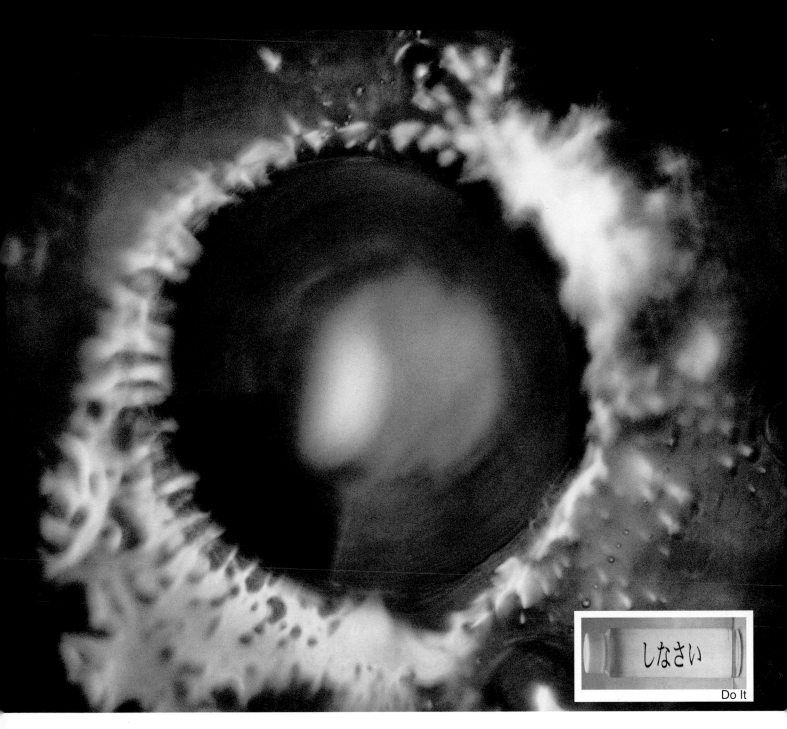

しなさい

Do It

Let's Do It/Do It

しようね・しなさい

「しなさい」という命令口調の言葉と、「しようね」という呼びかけの言葉の持つ意味の差が出ました。ついなんとなく毎日使っている言葉ですが、気軽に乱用することはできませんね。
話す相手に悪印象を与える意味が、こんなところにあったとは驚きです。

We wanted to see if a word that was commanding (such as, "Do it") and a word that was encouraging (such as, "Let's do it"), showed different results. These are words that we use everyday without thinking about it, but we should not abuse these words by using them too easily.
It is surprising to learn that meaning that give bad impression on the person you talk to existed in places like this.

きれい
Beautiful

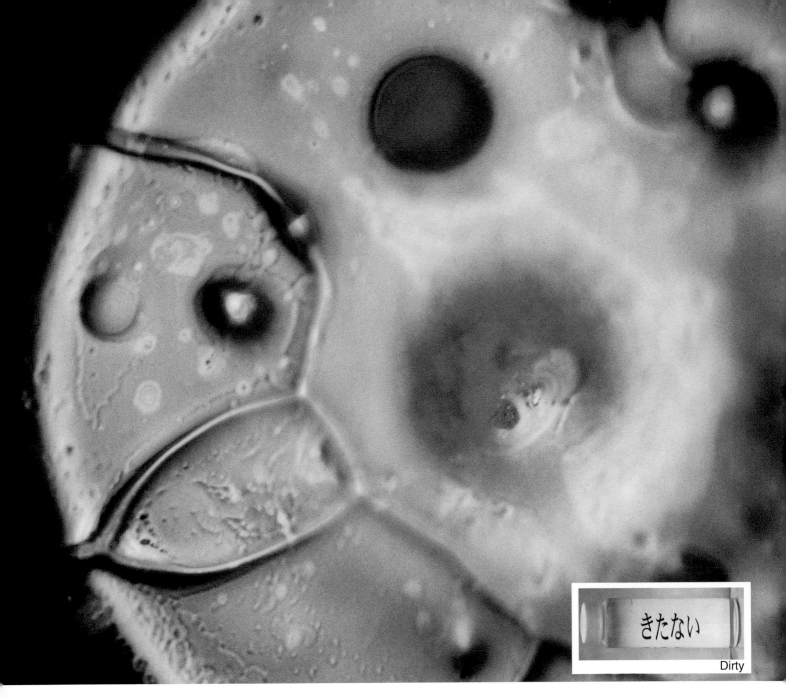

きたない

Dirty

Beautiful/Dirty
きれい・きたない

基本の水に「きれい」という文字を見せた水は美しい結晶に。「きたない」という文字を見せた水は、きたない結晶になってしまいました。私たちが考えている以上に、文字や言葉が水に対して、大きな影響力を持っていることを知らされる写真です。

The water that we exposed to the letters of "beautiful" developed a beautiful crystal and the water that we exposed to the word "Ugly" had ugly crystals. These pictures show, in more ways than we had imagined, that letters and words have a big influence on water crystals.

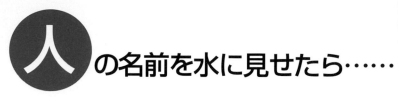

人の名前を水に見せたら……

感謝の気持ちを込めて

　また、とんでもないことを思いついた……と、撮影スタッフはびっくりしたようでした。なぜ、人の名前を水に見せたかというと、こんないきさつがありました。

　ある会社の経営者だったM氏が、波動を知ってから、2人の子どもたちと、社員が3人くらい波動を勉強するインストラクターになりました。そしてなんとなくギクシャクしていた家族の関係がとてもうまくいくようになった……ということで、私の研究に対して、大きなご協力をいただきました。

　このご好意に対して、どんなふうにお礼をしたらいいのかと、ずっと考えていました。そんなとき、ふっと『M氏の愛』という文字のラベルをつくって貼り、結晶写真をとってみました。すると予想以上に、100枚そろって、とてもきれいな結晶写真が撮れました。

　もう、うれしくて、額に入れてプレゼントしましたら、とても喜んでいただきました。

　それで今度は、お亡くなりになった人だったらいいかな……とか、たまたま講演に呼んでいただいて縁のある方や、気になる方を次々に試させていただきました。

　私自身、宗教にはまったくこだわっていませんし、実在の人なのか、神話の人なのかわからないような人もいますが……。

Showing Person's Name to Water

With Feeling of Gratitude

The photography staff was astonished when hearing of this idea. The reason why I decided to expose water to people's names is due to the following sequence of events.

When Mr. M, who was an executive of a company, learned about the properties of HADO two of his children and 3 employees became instructors in teaching the properties of HADO. Then their family relation, which was not going too well, improved. Because of this experience he was eager to cooperate in my research.

I had been wondering for sometime how I should thank him for his kindness. So, as a gift, I decided to paste a label on some samples of water that said, "Mr. M's love" and take a picture of the crystal that developed. Then, more than I had expected, all the 100 water samples developed into beautiful crystal pictures. I was so impressed that I put them in a frame and gave it to him as a present. Needless to say, it made him very happy. After that, I pasted the names of deceased people, the names of people who invited me to give lectures and names people who were on my mind.

I, myself am not devoted to any religion and some people cannot be distringuished whether they actually existed or their existence was just a myth.

Deguchi Onisaburo

でぐちおにさぶろう

出口王仁三郎

京都生まれで、出口ナオさんの娘さんとご結婚。新しい宗教の新しいかたちを考え、大本教を育てた方。力強い、独特のパワーを感じる結晶になりました。

Born in Kyoto, he married Deguchi Nao's daughter and created a religious association to try to raise the study of modern forms of religion.

Amaterasu Omikami

天照大神

あまてらすおおみかみ

日本の神様の中心的存在『天照大神』。予想にたがわず素晴らしい結晶でした。それぞれの枝の部分が神事に使う『御幣（ごへい）』のようにも見え、結晶の中は神の霊として祭られる『神鏡』のよう。中心から、うっすらと光が差してくるようにも感じられます。また最初の撮影から10秒後の写真を見ると、中心に日倫とも思える形が現われ、神鏡があるように結晶が成長していったのです。

Amaterasu Omikami is the most important Japanese God. A beautiful crystal developed as we imagined that it would.
Each branch of the crystal looks like the pendant paper strips that a Shinto shrine uses in its divine services. The center of crystal looks like the Divine Mirror as the Shinto religion calls God's spirit. I can feel light slightly shining out from the center. The shape like the sun appeared in the center of the crystal taken after 10 seconds from the first one. The crystal was developing and it had the shape that looked like Divine Mirror.

撮影10秒後、成長する結晶
Developing crystal 10 seconds after photographing

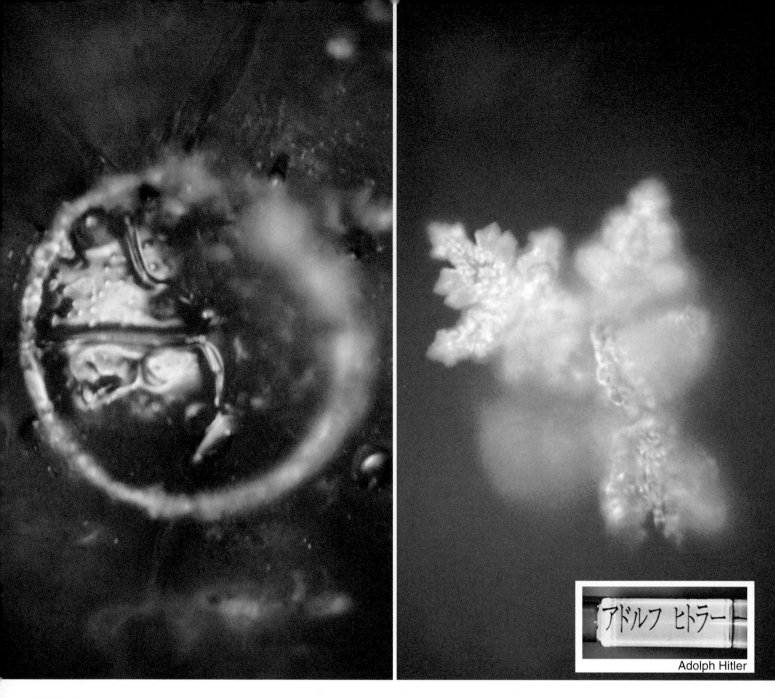

Adolph Hitler

アドルフ・ヒトラー

大量殺戮を繰り返した『ヒトラー』の文字を見せた結晶は「ムカツク・殺す」の場合と似ています。しかしほんの数枚ですが、右のような写真も撮れました。結晶にはなっていませんが、結晶化しようとしている様子が感じられます。これを見ると世の中には根っからの悪人など存在せず、誰もが良心を持っている存在でないかと思え、希望が持てます。

The crystal of water to which we exposed to the name "Hitler," looks like that of the water that we exposed to the words "You make me sick" and "I will kill you" too. However, we also had a few pictures like those shown right (though the number was small). The sample did not form a complete crystal, but it seems like it is trying to crystallize. When we look at this, we can infer that there are no truly wicked persons in humans because everyone has conscience.

マザーテレサ
Mother Teresa

Mother Teresa
マザーテレサ

世界中の人の応援を受けて、インドで一部の恵まれない人々のために、貢献の一生を送った方。
ノーベル平和賞をうける栄誉を博しました。テレサさん、若いころにはこんなお顔だったかも……。

She is a person who devoted her life to the underprivileged people in India and has received support from all over the world for her efforts. She was also honored to be awarded The Nobel Peace Prize. Mother Teresa may have looked like this when she was young.

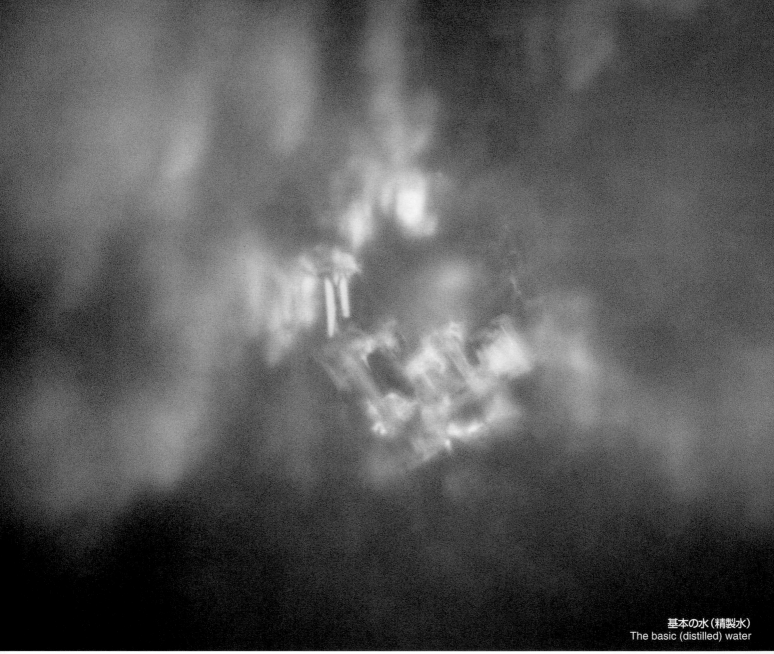

Placing Water on a Picture
水を写真の上に置いたら……

文字ではなく、水に写真を見せたらどうなるのかという実験です。
幼い子どもの笑顔の写真の上に、基本の水を置いて変化をみました。
結晶の枝の部分が大きく元気良く伸びている様子は、見る人をホッとさせてくれます。

This is an experiment in which we exposed water to pictures instead of to words. We placed a picture of a toddler's smiling face on a sample of our basic distilled water. The branch part of the crystal stretches out energetically. People have commented that it gives them the impression of being relaxed.

写真の上に水を置いて
Place water on the picture

基本の水（精製水）に無邪気な子どもの写真を見せたら
Water crystal after exposing the picture of the innocent child to the basic (distilled) water

第三章 江本勝・水の世界は拡がる！

『波動・気』とは

　すべての物質は、物質のモトである１つ以上の原子の組み合わせによってできています。その原子は電子と原子核とで構成されています。電子はマイナス、原子核はプラスであるために、電子は原子核の周りを超高速でシフトしながら、それぞれ固有の微弱な振動波を発しています。これを私は『波動』と呼んでいます。

　波動は電気的な引き合いによって、激しいスピードであっちこっちに動きます。この動きが模様（パターン・共鳴磁場）をつくるのですが、同じものはひとつもありません。これを現代科学では『カオス』とか『混沌（こんとん）』といい表わすようになりました。

　原子レベルまでは規則性がありますが、原子をつくる素粒子は現代科学の世界においてもあいまいな存在であるといわれています。私が思うに、それはなぜかというと、観測する人の意識、モノの見方によって変わる……。その世界は人間の意識レベルと同等のレベルであるからだと思っています。

　ですから物質の根源のレベルは、人の意識によって左右されることになります。つまり、どんなことも人の意識によって形づくられていると考えています。

　波動はとても重要なエネルギーであるのに、目に見えないがために、一般の科学の発展からは置き去りにされていました。

　私は門外漢です。

　そして、おそらく専門外の位置にいるからこそ、波動というエネルギーを、「水という素材・キャンバスを使って目に見えるように表現しよう」という発想に至ることができたのだと思います。

　波動の原理を応用すると、たとえば生命体の健康状態、心の安定度、水の良し悪しや状態など、さまざまなものの様子が手にとるようにわかります。

　波動は、目に見えないエネルギーの最小単位ですが、身近にある音波も電波も『波動』の一種です。

　中学の理科の時間で行った音叉の実験を思い出してください。同じ周波数の音叉を２つ並べて、片方の音叉を鳴らすと、まったく手を触れていない方の音叉に振動が伝わり、それを共震させます。これを『共鳴』といいますが、共鳴によるエネルギーの伝達方法は、テレビ、ラジオ、携帯電話にも利用されています。

　私たちの身の回りには実際に『波動』を利用した技術が数多く活躍しているのです。

Chapter 3 Masaru Emoto/The World of Water Spreads Afar

What Is HADO/Chi?

All substances are composed of combinations of atoms. Atoms are composed of electrons and an atomic nucleus. Because electrons are negative and the atomic nucleus is positive, electrons orbit around the atomic nucleus at an ultra high speed and emit unique, faint vibration waves. This is what we call HADO.

The HADO moves around at an intense speed by electrons electrically pulling against each other. This motion forms a pattern (Magnetic Resonance Field), of which there are not two alike. This is what is called "Chaos" in modern science.

There is regularity in the atomic nucleus level, but the elementary particle that is found is atoms has no regularity in modern science. The reason is that it changes according to the consciousness of observers, by the way they see things. The world of the neutrino is at the same consciousness level as that of human beings.

That is why the root level of matter depends on people's consciousness.

Despite the fact that HADO is a very important phenomenon, it has been neglected in the development of general science, simply because it is invisible.

I am an outsider. I am not in a professional position. So I am actually at an advantage, and I could obtain the idea to try to put HADO energy into "a visible form by using water crystals as material and canvas."

When we apply the principle the intensity of wave motion for instance, the health and stability of a creature's mind (good or bad) as well as the condition of the water can affect the process.

HADO is the minimum unit of invisible energy. Sound and electricity also have HADO.

Try to remember back to the tuning fork experiment that you did in your science class in junior high. You placed two tuning forks of the same frequency in line and then sounded one tuning fork. The sound was transmitted to the other tuning fork and resonated without making contact. This is called resonance.

This method of energy transmission through resonance is used in televisions, radios and cellular phones.

There are many things around us that actually make use of HADO technology.

『波動』を測定する機械『ＭＲＡ』

　それぞれの物質がもつ、固有のエネルギーパターンをコード化し、共鳴するかしないかを調べることによって、さまざまな波動の状態を測定することができる機械が、12年ほど前にアメリカで開発されました。波動の測定を可能にしたその機械の名前は、『ＭＲＡ＝Magnetic Resonance Analyzer（共鳴磁場分析器）』といいます。

　そしてそれを日本にはじめて持ち込んだのが、私こと江本勝です。

　ここで「水が情報を記憶する」という技術と、私たちが研究してきた「波動」技術がドッキングしました。そして「波動と水」の研究をはじめて、すでに11年の歳月が過ぎ、11冊の本を出版し（6ページ参照）、なかにはベストセラーになるなどの経験もさせていただきました。

Measuring Machine of "HADO"

A machine, "MRA (Magnetic Resonance Analyzer)," which measures various states of HADO, encodes the unique energy pattern of each substance and checks whether it resonates or not, has been developed in the USA for the first time in the world 12 years ago.
This machine that makes the measurement of HADO possible is called the Magnetic Resonance Analyzer (MRA).
The saving/storing information and the wave motion technology that I had been doing research on united.
In the 11 years since I started my research on "HADO and Water," I have published 11 books, some of which have become best-sellers.
(Please reter to page 6.)

人工的に水を変える『転写技術』

水に『波動』情報を転写する技術の開発

後述（133ページ）の船井幸雄先生は、ご自身のやり方で『愛の気』を水に加えられ転写されましたが、私のような普通の人間には、こんなことができるとは思えません。

そこで『MRA』という『波動・気』を測定するコンピュータの出番です。

MRAをはじめとする波動測定器（現在、波動を計る機械は国産のものも含め、かなりの種類があります）には、必ず波動転写機能が備わっています。測定はまず、測定器が微弱な共鳴磁場を出力し、それが被験者や物質に発信され、共鳴の有無を確認します。また測定器の出力部分を増強することによって、波動情報を転写することもできるのです。

そして転写の相手は『水』。それは水がもっとも情報の保持能力が高いからです。

水道水やダムの水に対しても、MRAで免疫のコード（正常な免疫力の波動情報）を転写、撮影を試みました。

免疫力の高い水の結晶は、必ずしっかりとした亀の甲の形をしていることも、多くの結晶写真を撮るあいだに確信することができました。

また、同じ水に同じ情報を転写した場合、いつ、何回やっても同じ傾向をもつ結晶写真ができることも明らかになりました。

従来の科学的分析法なら、成分的にまったく変化のない水も、結晶写真にしてはじめて、大きな変化として読み取っていただけるようになりました。

万病に効くということで、アマゾン川の奥地などでは、多くの人々が薬になる木々を伐採しているといいます。でも、この転写技術が公に認められ、少しの情報を水に転写することによって効力を発揮することが理解されれば、環境保護にも一役をかうことでしょう。

その日が早く来ることを願ってやみません。

"Transcript Technology" that Changes Water Artificially

Development of Technology of Transcribing HADO

Mr. Yukio Funai, mentioned on page 133, added the spirit of love to water in his own way for transcription. I didn't think another layman like I could do such a thing.

HADO measuring instruments, including the MRA (currently, there are many types of HADO measuring instruments, including some domestic models), have HADO transcribing functions. The measurement first starts when the MRA puts out a faint resonance magnetic field, which is then transmitted to the subject and substances to be measured. Then the existence of resonance is checked. By amplifying the output of the measuring instrument HADO information can be transcribed.

The information is transcribed on to water because water has the highest retention capacity of information.

We also tried transcribing and photographing an immunity code (HADO information of normal immune strength) on to tap water and dam water with the MRA. After taking many crystal pictures we confirmed that crystals of water that have a high immune strength always have a firm tortoiseshell form.

It was made clear that when we transcribed the same information on to the same type of water, we obtained crystal pictures that had the same tendencies.

We were able to prove that a big change could be seen in pictures of water crystals that we had taken when no change was evident after the same crystals were studied through conventional scientific analysis methods.

We hear that trees at the upper reaches of the Amazon River are being logged for their potential cure-all effects as drugs. This transcription technology is approved by people. However, if those same people were to understand the effects of transcribing this kind of information, I know that it would help them to affect environmental protection laws. I wish such day will come soon.

品川区の水道水に
免疫情報を転写

　東京の品川の水道水に、ＭＲＡで免疫のコード・波動情報を転写して、水の変化を撮影しました。左の基本の水は東京の水道水ですが、結晶にはほど遠いグロテスクな状態です。それが同じ水とは思えないほど明らかに変化しています。

　このような変化が見られる理由としては、何らかのエネルギーが水に加わったと考えるのが自然です。それが私たちがいう「波動」。しかもＭＲＡという波動測定器から発せられるエネルギーパターンには類似性があり、ある程度同じような形の結晶が得られるということも付け加えておきます。

　たとえば免疫波動を転写して、何種類もの水で調べましたが、123ページのカルチャー200に見られるように、典型的な免疫の形である、素晴らしい亀の甲型の結晶が得られています。

免疫情報を入れる前の品川の水道水
Tap water in Shinagawa before giving immune information

Transcribing Change and Immune Information on the Tap Water of Shinagawa-ku

We took a picture of change occurring in water by transcribing the HADO information of an immune code with the MRA on to a tap water sample from Shinagawa, Tokyo. The unaltered water on the left is the tap water of Tokyo. Its crystal formation is so grotesque. This second picture shows change to such an extent that it cannot be believed that it is the same water as was used for the first crystal.

It is natural to think that some kind of energy was applied to the water for such change to take place. This is what we call HADO. I would like to add that there is a similarity in the energy patterns emitted from a HADO measuring instrument, the MRA, as shown by the fact that the 2 crystals are of the same shape to a certain degree.

For instance, we transcribed a immune HADO, and did a survey using many types of water. As can be seen in culture 200 on page 123, we were able to obtain a wonderful tortoise-shell shaped crystal.

免疫情報を入れた後の品川の水道水
Tap water of Shinagawa after giving immune information

リー・H・ロレンツェン博士の「マイクロクラスター水」

リー・H・ロレンツェン博士夫妻
Doctor and Mrs. Lee H. Lorenzen

すべては夫人のために

私が水の研究をはじめるキッカケとなった人で、その後も指導を仰いでいるアメリカのリー・H・ロレンツェン博士は、このマイクロクラスター化された水が情報を保持・記憶することに着目し、科学的に証明した第一人者です。

リー・H・ロレンツェン博士は、産婦人科医の息子。

学生を集めて、勉強をしながら世界各国を何ヵ月かけて廻るという『洋上大学』に参加し、そこで運命の出会いをしました。同じメンバー（レーガン大統領時の法務長官ビル・スミス氏の娘さん）に恋をしたのです。そして、はじめてデートをしたのが日本の神戸。めでたく結婚しましたが、夫人は病弱でした。

できるかぎりのことをしようと、あらゆる病院を探し、どんなに腕のいいといわれる医師を見つけて治療しても、なかなか良くならなかった夫人。あるとき博士は人間の身体の中で60〜70％を占めるという水に着目します。
「身体の中の水を変えてみたらどうだろうか」

そこで夫人のために水の開発をはじめました。

「マイクロクラスター水」とは

水は通常、ひとつひとつの分子が単独で存在するのではなく、水素結合し、クラスターと呼ばれる小さな水の粒の集団を形成しています。そして、この水の分子を整列させて、小さくすることを水をクラスター化するといいます。

クラスター化された水は、小回りがきき、身体の隅々まで行き渡り、細胞への吸収力も高いというわけです。生物、科学、農業にも使えるこれらの水のことを、総称して『機能水・波動水』とも呼んでいます。

研究のすえ、蒸留水を循環させながらレーザーを通して、水に特定の磁場を加え、水を強力に結合させることに成功。しかも、その水に、ある物質のもつ情報をプリント、転写する方法を確立しました。この情報を転写された水は、'98年1月、アメリカで特許を得て「マイクロクラスター水」と呼ばれています。

水は情報を持って、しかも運ぶ役目をしているわけですから、人間にとって良い水とは「身体にとって良い情報を保持し、必要な場所に運搬することのできる、マイクロクラスター化された水」です。「美味しい水が五臓六腑にしみわたる」というのは、まさにこのことです。

博士のこの水の開発によって、夫人は健康を取り戻すことができたのです。

リー・H・ロレンツェン博士の開発した「マイクロクラスター水」は、現在メキシコやアメリカの医師たちの協力を得て臨床実験が重ねられ、多くの実績をあげています。この分野の研究が進めば、21世紀は「水と薬が共生する時代」がくるでしょう。

The Micro-cluster Water of Dr. Lee H. Lorenzen

All for His Wife

The person who first introduced me to the idea of doing research on water (and who I still receive guidance from) was Dr. Lee H. Lorenzen. He is a recognized authority who has directed his attention to the study of micro-clustered water's information retaining and storing capacities and has proven much of his research scientifically.

Dr. Lee H. Lorenzen is a son of an obstetrician and gynecologist. He was among the students who participated in the Marine College which is a college that provides courses to its students while they travel around the world for a few months. During the voyage, he fell deeply in love with another student (the daughter of Attorney General in the Reagan administration). They had their very first date in Kobe, Japan. They got married but his wife had been weak.

He tried to do everything that he could including visiting many hospitals in search a good doctor to treat her. She would not recover from her illness despite his efforts. One day his attention was directed to the fact that water accounts for 60 to 70% of the human weight.

How about changing the water in the body?

He started developing water for his beloved wife.

What is Micro-cluster Water?

Water normally is not composed of independent molecules, but rather they are hydrogen bonded to form small water particles called clusters.

When you align these water molecules and make them smaller it is called clustering.

Clustered water can easily make sharp turns and subsequently can reach far into the corners of the body. Its absorption power in the cells is very high.

Water that can be used in biology, science and agriculture is generally called "Functional water/HADO water."

As a result of our research, he has succeeded in making water more powerful circulating distilled water through a laser beam while adding a special magnetic field. He also established a method of printing and transcribing the information that a certain substance has.

In January, 1998 in the USA, a patent was obtained for water to which this information is transcribed, and it is called Micro-cluster water.

Water carries information and at the same time has a transporting role. So good water means "Micro-clustered water that can retain information is good for the body and transport the information to the necessary places." This is what we mean when we say ,"Good water pervades in five viscera and six entrails".

With the development of this water by Dr. Lorenzen, his wife recovered her health.

"Micro-cluster water", developed by Dr. Lee H. Lorenzen, has undergone various clinical experiments with the cooperation of doctors in Mexico and USA, and is achieving many good results. If research in this field progresses, the 21st century will be an age where "Water lives in symbiosis with medicine."

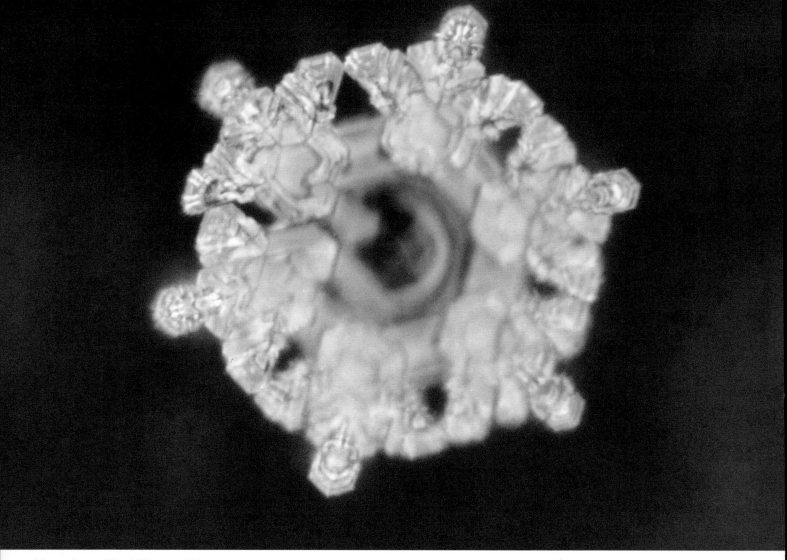

Micro-cluster Water/Culture 200

マイクロクラスター水・**カルチャー200**

リー・Ｈ・ロレンツェン博士が開発した水のひとつ。コーカサス（ロシア南部）地方は世界的に長寿村として有名で、100歳を超える人々が多く住んでいます。長寿の要因のひとつと言われ、彼等が愛飲している山羊の乳からつくった乳酸菌飲料の情報を転写したもの。この乳酸菌（ケフィア菌）は移動させると菌の性質が変わってしまうのですが、その情報だけを取り出して転写すれば、同じ効果が得られます。この情報を転写した水の結晶写真は、非常に形の整った基本的な亀の甲の形をしています。つまり免疫の形である六角構造で、情報をしっかり保持していることを現わしています。200倍に希釈して飲みます。

This is one of the kinds of water developed by Dr. Lee H Lorenzen. The Caucasus region of southern Russia is world famous as a region where many people live to an advanced age. There are many people there who are over 100 years old. This is a picture of water crystals transcribed with the information from a lactic acid drink made from goat milk that they habitually drink. This lactic acid (Kefia bacteria) changes its property when it is transferred, but if we take out only its information and transcribe it, we can obtain the same effect. A crystal picture of water transcribed with this information has a very organized and basic tortoise-shell shape. In other words, it is of a hexagonal structure, an immunized shape, and shows that it retains information well. For drinking, it is diluted by 200-fold.

マイクロクラスター水・アンデス400

アンデス（南米）地方に自生し、万病に効くという『キャッツクロー（＝クラクラ）』という樹の樹液エキスの情報を、レーザー処理して転写した水の結晶写真です。
基本の水は蒸留水ですが、見事に整った美しい形に変化しています。
ちなみに400の意味は、400倍に希釈して飲む飲み方を示しています。

This is a picture of water to which the information of a resin extract called Cat's claw (Kurakura) is laser treated and transcribed. Cat's claw naturally grows in the Andes region of South America and is an effective treatment or panacea.
The initial water sample was a distilled water but its crystal has changed into an organized beautiful shape.
The word 400 means that for drinking it is diluted 400-fold.

ダムの源水
Source water in dam

転写後
After transcription

埼玉県・ちちぶ湖　二瀬ダムの水に
波動情報を転写

　現在のダムは、どこもよどんだ水にアオコが多く、酸性化が進んでいます。ダムは、本来滔々と流れているはずの水を溜めているという不自然な状態にあります。

　これでは、ダムの周辺の生体系を壊し、酸性化したまま下流に流れていく水によって、周辺の汚染がすすみ、自然破壊に向かっていくしかありません。

　とにかくダムの水を良くしたい……と思い、ダムの水に必要な波動情報を転写すると、美しい結晶がとれました。

　大きな転写装置をつくり、発展させれば、ダムの水も良くなるはずだと確信しています。

　ところで、ダムの結晶写真を撮影中に、思いがけない写真が撮れました。

　次ページの写真は5秒ごとにシャッターを切ったものですが、連写をはじめたときの写真と、5秒後の写真で、緑の部分と赤い部分が、反転しています。

　これがどういう意味をもっているのか、今のところよくわかりません。

　将来への課題としたいと思っています。

Transcription of HADO Information onto Futase Dam of Chichibu Lake, Saitama Prefecture

Most of the present dams are stagnant where many Aoko (blue green algae) live and acidification at these dams is progressing. The dam stops water from flowing swiftly, thus keeping the water in an unnatural state.
This disrupts the ecosystem on the periphery of the dam. The water then flows down river in an acidified form, contaminating the vicinity and destroying nature.
While harboring earnest feelings for its improvement, we transcribed the necessary wave motion to the dam water. As a result we came out with a picture of a beautiful crystal.
We are confident that if we make and develop a large transcribing device we can improve dam water.
By the way, during the photographing of the dam crystal pictures we also came out with an unexpected picture.
The pictures on the next page were taken every 5 seconds and you can see that the first picture and the picture taken 5 seconds later have reversed red and green areas.
We do not know what this means but this will be a future topic of study for us.

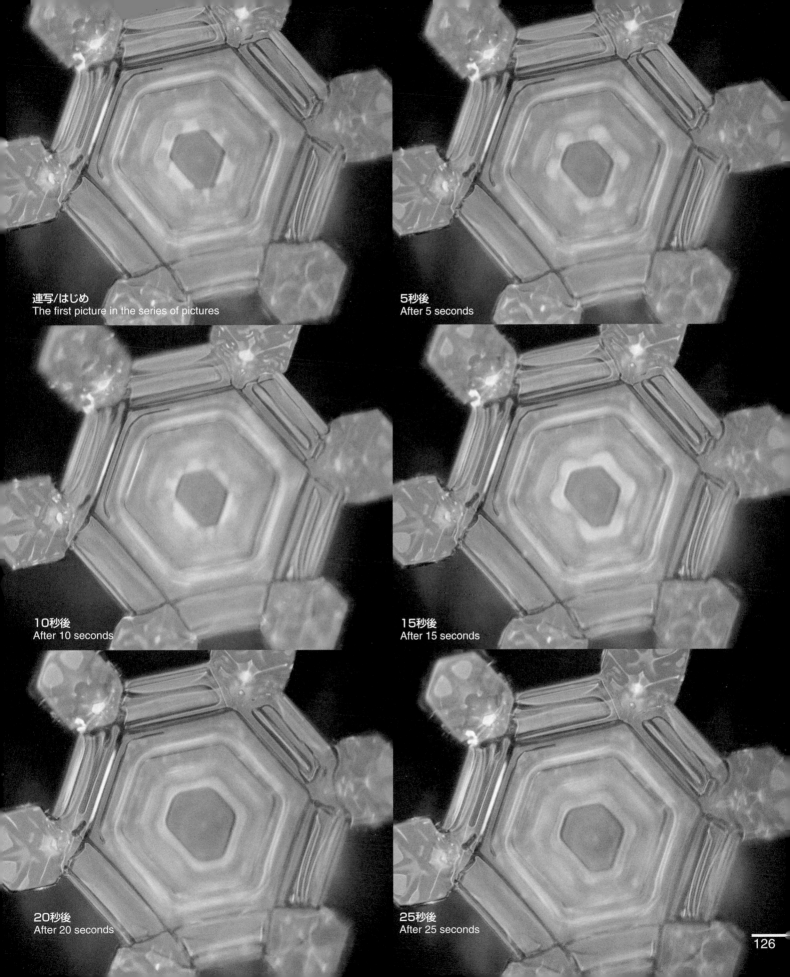

連写/はじめ
The first picture in the series of pictures

5秒後
After 5 seconds

10秒後
After 10 seconds

15秒後
After 15 seconds

20秒後
After 20 seconds

25秒後
After 25 seconds

カモミール
Camomile

アロマオイルの情報を
水に転写
〜カモミール水、フェンネル水〜

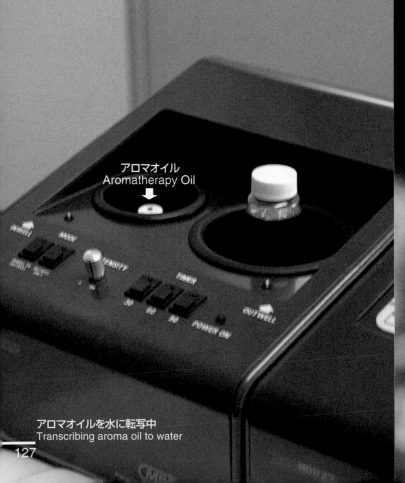
アロマオイル
Aromatherapy Oil

アロマオイルを水に転写中
Transcribing aroma oil to water

カモミール水の結晶写真
Crystal picture of camomile water

127

フェンネル
Fennel

アロマオイルのもっている波動情報を、水に転写して凍らせ、結晶写真にしたものです。
アロマオイルになる前の、もともとの花によく似た結晶が得られ、とてもびっくりしました。
結晶というものは、その物質がもつ形の相似性といえるのかもしれません。

HADO information that aromatherapy oil contains was transcribed to a water sample and was frozen before taking the crystal's picture.
We were surprised to obtain a picture of a crystal that is similar to the look of the flowers that the different aroma oils were made from.
These crystals may resemble the shape of the substance.

フェンネル水の結晶写真
Crystal picture of Fennel water

人 の意識で変わる水

水は人の意識を写す

「水に文字を見せる」という試みは、私たちの予想を超える成果をもたらせてくれました。ここまで、水に音楽を聴かせたり、文字を見せたり、名前を見せたりしてきて、非常に楽しい体験をすることができました。

この実験の成果によって、文字や写真という「形」によっても情報が伝えられるという仮説が得られたように思います。

結晶がここまで大きな、はっきりとした変化を見せてくれるとは予想できませんでした。水が情報を記憶し、伝えることができるということがわかってきたのです。

このような結果を得ると、どうしても人の意識が水にどのような変化を与えるのだろうか……という領域に踏み込みたくなってきました。

それは、じつは4年前の悲しい、つらい出来事からスタートしました。あの阪神・淡路大震災の直後、私の手元に送られてきた神戸の水の結晶写真は、大いに人の意識を内在するようなものであったからです。その証拠に3ヵ月後には、同じ神戸の水が劇的に変わってしまったからです。

人の意識によって、変化した水の結晶写真をご紹介させていただきます。

Water Changed by People's Consciousness

Water Reflects People's Consciousness

Our attempt at exposing water to language had greater results than we had expected. So far, we had very interesting experiences with exposing water to music, to language and to names. With the results of this experiment, we were able to formulate a hypothesis that information can be transmitted through "Shapes" such as words and pictures.

We did not expect though, that the crystals would show such dramatic and clear changes. We have become aware that water stores and transmits information.

After obtaining results like this, we could not resist stepping into the territory of human consciousness? We wanted to find out what kind of change thought could cause.

The idea started after a sad and painful experience that we had four years ago. Immediately after the Great Hanshin-Awaji Earthquake, the crystal pictures of the water from Kobe had something greatly inherent in human consciousness. To prove this, 3 months afterwards, the water in Kobe changed greatly.

We would like to show the crystal picture changed by people's consciousness.

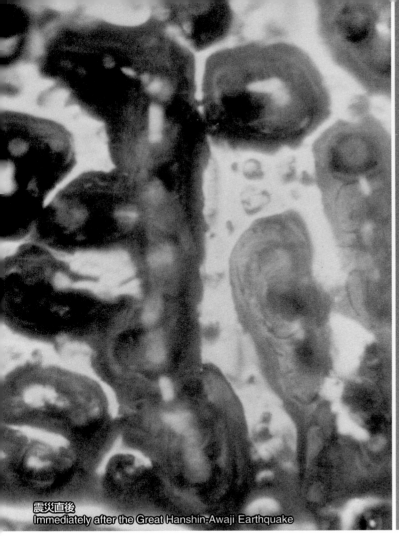

震災直後
Immediately after the Great Hanshin-Awaji Earthquake

震災3ヵ月後
3 months after the Earthquake

The Great Hanshin-Awaji Earthquake and Tap Water

阪神・淡路大震災と水道水

　1995年1月17日、阪神・淡路地方を襲った大震災の3日後、神戸で採取した、たまたま出ていた水道水の結晶写真です。

　震災直後の人々の「恐怖やパニック、深い悲しみ」を水がキャッチしたかのよう……。結晶はメチャクチャに壊れ、見る人の気持ちまでゾッとさせるような写真になりました。あまりの悲惨さに、公開はできないと思いました。

　ところが3ヵ月後……。打ちのめされた神戸の人々に、世界中から援助の手が差し伸べられ、世界中の人が思いを寄せました。暴動が起きなかったことで、思いもかけず、日本人はすばらしいとさえいわれました。

　山のように積み上げられたガレキのなかで、人々は人間のやさしさ、温かさを取り戻すことができた……そんな思いや願いが重なる結晶です。

On January 17, 1995, the Great Hanshin-Awaji Earthquake occurred in Kobe. Three days afterwards we took pictures of the crystals found in the tap water in Kobe (that was available at that time). It is as if the water captured the fear, panic and deep sorrow of the people immediately after the earthquake. The crystals were completely destroyed. It was a picture that made people shudder.
We felt that we could not make this public because of the horror of its extreme misery.
However, 3 months after that... Helping hands and sympathy from all over the world were given to the people of Kobe. Also since no riots occurred the people of Kobe were praised by many people.
Although the rubble piled up high, people were able to restore their environment due the kindness and warmth of others. This crystal seems to have collected these feelings also.

500人の『愛の気・言魂(言霊)』を受けた水

日本全国にいる500人の波動インストラクター（私が主催する波動学の卒業生たち）に手紙を出しました。

1997年2月2日午後2時、オフィスの私の机の上に、東京品川の水道水を入れたコップを置いておきます。それに対して、みなさんの想いを発信してください。

もちろん、この水が良い水になるように。「水がきれいになりました。ありがとうございました」という願いを込めて、各地から、同時刻に、愛の『気・言魂』を送ってください。

こうして、全国から愛の『気・言魂』を送ってもらった結果の結晶写真（右ページ参照）です。もちろん、物理的な変化は何ひとつ加えていません。

予想はしていたものの、これほど見事な変化を得られたことに対して、撮影班一同、感動を通り越して涙がこぼれそうになってしまいました。

▲元の水　東京品川の水道水　前日撮影
Original water
The picture of tap water in Shinagawa, Tokyo taken the day before

改めて協力していただいた全国の皆さんに感謝します。そして、人の想いのパワーは、距離に関係なく届くと思えるようになったのです。

Water with "Chi, Soul and Spirit" of 500 people

I sent letters to 500 HADO instructors across Japan (graduates of my HADO study). "At 2:00 on February 2, 1997, I will leave a cup containing the tap water of Shinagawa-ku on the table in my office. Please transmit your feelings to that water at the same time from all over Japan. Of course, for this water to become a clean water, please send "Chi and Soul" of love and the wish that the water should become clean. Thank you very much."
In this way, water received "Chi and Soul" from all over Japan. And this is the picture of crystal we obtained. (Please refer to the right page.)
Of course, no physical change was made.
We had not expected it but were able to obtain a clear change in the condition of the water. All of the staff were so impressed that they were almost ready to cry. We feel deeply appreciative of all those who cooperated with us from all over Japan. We started to feel that people's thoughts could be gathered regardless of how far apart they are.

500人の愛の気を受けた水の結晶
Water with "Chi, Soul and Spirit" of 500 People

船井氏の愛の気を受けた水

　東京品川の水道水に、日頃からご理解をいただいている船井総合研究所の船井幸雄先生に、『愛の気』を加えていただいた水の結晶写真です。当然良い結晶がとれるという想いはありましたが、正直、もとが水道水だから……これほどきれいな結晶が得られるとは思っていませんでした。

　この結晶は、それまでのどの映像よりも美しいものでした。人間の意識が、浄水器などの機械を使うより、はるかに素晴らしく、緻密で美しい結晶をつくる水に変化させることができたのです。

　水は心を反映させる……『水は心の鏡』という昔からある言葉を証明する結晶写真になったと思います。

　これが可能だとすれば、心配されている水道水を、それを扱う人の意識によって、ここまで美しい結晶ができる水に変えることも不可能ではありません。

　そしてこのことは、人間がちょっとした行為や言葉で、水を美しく良い水にすることができるに違いないということも教えてくれているような気がします。

Water with Mr. Funai's "Chi of Love"

This is a picture of a crystal of a tap water sample from Shinagawa-ku, Tokyo, that Mr. Yukio Funai of Funai Consulting Co., Ltd., (a supporter of our research) applied "Chi of Love" to. I felt without doubt that we could obtain well-formed crystals. However, because it was originally only ordinary tap water, we did not really expect that we could obtain such a beautiful crystal.
This is called, "Water is the mirror of mind."
If this is possible, then it could also be possible to change controversial tap water to a beautiful crystal through the conscious thought of human beings.
And this fact seems to indicate that our actions and words make water more beautiful and cleaner.

と言魂について

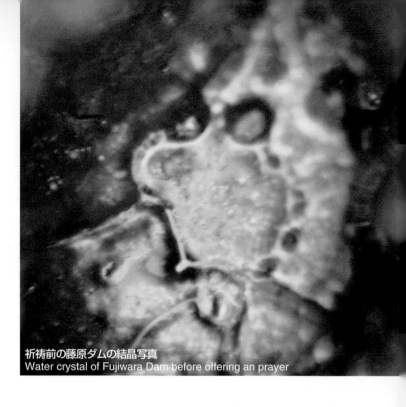

祈祷前の藤原ダムの結晶写真
Water crystal of Fujiwara Dam before offering an prayer

人の意識と結晶

　最後にひとつ。これは群馬県の水上町にある藤原ダムで行われた、大宮市寿宝院の加藤宝喜住職の「言魂による水の浄化実験」の結果得られた結晶写真です。

　日本では古くから、言葉に魂が宿るといわれ、言魂（ことだま）の考え方は広く浸透しています。

　実験前のダムの水の結晶写真は、なんともおぞましい限りで、もだえくるしむ人の顔のようにも見えます。この日、加藤住職は、ダムのほとりで、約1時間にわたって、加持祈祷の業を行われました。業が終了して、しばらくした後に、その場に立ち合った私たちが肉眼でもわかるほど、ダムの水が見る見るキレイになりました。これを目のあたりにして、非常にびっくりし、たいへん感動しました。

　さらに結晶写真ではどうだろうと、期待を込めて持ち返って撮影したものが、表紙でもご紹介している結晶写真です。

　今までにこれほど美しく、本当に光り輝くエネルギーを発している写真は見たことがありません。六角構造の中に、さらに小さな六角形があり、その回りを取り巻く光のオブジェは、オーラでもあり、中央の三日月型の部分は、まるで後光が差しているかのようでもあります。

　人の意識に基づく言魂のエネルギーの計り知れないパワーを感じさせる写真であり、人間の愛や感謝に基づくエネルギーと水とが調和したとき、とてつもなく素晴らしいことが起こるのではないでしょうか。

Water and Soul

People's Consciousness and Crystals

Lastly, this is a picture of a crystal of water obtained as a result of a water purification experiment "through soul" by Reverend Kato Hoki, the chief priest of Jyuhouin Temple, Omiya City. The experiment was conducted at the Fujiwara Dam in Minakami-cho, Gunma Prefecture.
In Japan, it is widely believed that the soul dwells in the spirit which is present in words.
The picture of the crystal of water before the experiment, is indeed horrifying and in fact has the appearance of the face of a person who is suffering great agony. The day of the experiment, Reverend Kato, performed a prayer practice for 1 hour beside the dam. Moments after the practice ended, the dam water became visibly beautiful. We observed this with our own eyes and were very astonished as well as very impressed.
How does the crystal picture look? We took pictures of the crystals with great expectations and we obtained crystal pictures as beautiful as the one on the cover.
We have never seen a beautiful picture that emits brilliant energy as much as this one does. Amidst the basic hexagonal structure, there is a also a small hexagon. This hexagon is an object d'art of light that is surrounded by an aura. The crescent portion at the center also seems to have a halo around it.
People say that this picture makes them feel an immeasurable amount of power and energy in their soul based on people's consciousness. When energy based on people's love and appreciation harmonizes with water, why should such a wonderful thing seem so unreasonable?

祈祷前ダムに波がでる
Waving water in dam before praying

祈祷後に波が静止した
Still water in dam after praying

祈祷後湖水がきれいに
Water of the lake became clear after praying

祈祷後
After offering a prayer

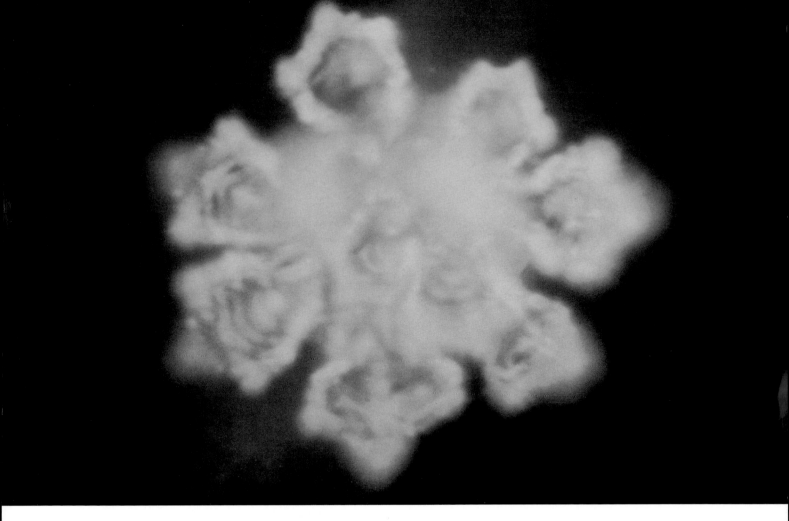

七角形の結晶写真が撮れました！

We Could Take a Heptagonal Crystal Picture

　加藤住職の祈祷のときの藤原ダム水を滴下して撮影すると、ほとんどが表紙と前ページのような素晴らしい写真になりました。

　さらにその中に数枚、不思議な写真が撮れました。その１つをご紹介いたします。

　美しさの点では、表紙の写真にまさるものではありませんが、よく見ると、なんと六角形ではなく、七角形になっているのです。今までに七角形の結晶は一度も撮れたことがありません。加藤住職は七弁財天さんにお願いをされたのだとか。

　水はいろいろの伝言をもたらしてくれていますが、伝言を聴くわれわれ人間の方が、大いに勉強する必要があるようです。

We were taking pictures of the dripping water of Fujiwara Dam while Reverend Kato was giving prayers. During that shoot we obtained pictures of crystals as wonderful as those on the cover page.

Among them, we were able to obtain a few mysterious pictures of which this is one.

In terms of beauty, there is nothing that compares to the one on the cover. Take a close look and you will be astonished to find that it is not a hexagon but a heptagon. We had never been able to obtain a picture of a heptagonal crystal before this experience. Reverend Kato said he prayed to the Seven Benzaiten (Goddesses of Fortune).

Water has a variety of messages, but it seems that we have a lot to learn from messages we receive.

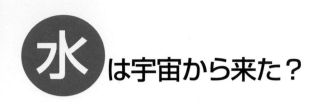

水は宇宙から来た？

水の不思議は深まるばかり

結晶写真による水の評価方法は、従来の科学的な分析評価法とはまったく違う視点からの新しいアプローチです。

そして実験を続けてわかったことは、「水」に関しては私たちはやはり、まだほとんど何もわかっていないということ。

疑問や課題がどんどん拡がっています。

まず地球上に存在する水。

この水はなぜあるのでしょう。水の起源については、今まで謎に包まれていました。しかし宇宙探査が進んでくるに従って、かつて火星にも水があったらしいことも確認されています。水は少なくとも地球固有のものではなく、宇宙にくまなく存在することがわかってきたようです。

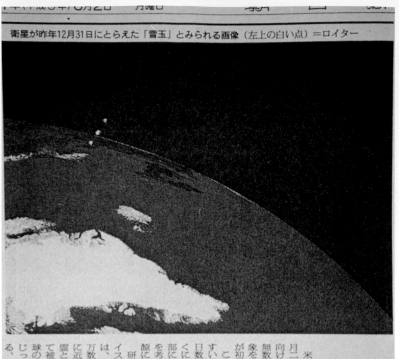

衛星が昨年12月31日にとらえた「雪玉」とみられる画像（左上の白い点）＝ロイター

宇宙から「雪玉」
海水の供給源だった？
NASAが観測・発表

米航空宇宙局（NASA）は五月二十八日、宇宙から地球大気に向けて雪の玉のような微小天体が無数に飛来しているとみられる現象を米国の極地観測衛星ポーラーが初めて観測した、と発表した。

この雪玉は直径十数分の小さすい星のような天体とみられ、毎日数千も飛来するが、地表に近づくにつれて分解し、やがて雲の一部になる。地球誕生以降の長い間、海の水の重要な供給源になった可能性があるという。

研究グループのアイオワ大のルイス・フランク博士らの分析では、この天体は地上約千キロから二万数千キロ上空で小さく分解。地表に近づくにつれて太陽光を浴びて雲となる。このため、地上に落ちて被害を及ぼすことはないが、地球の大気循環により生じる雲と混じって、宇宙由来の雨を降らせる、という。

フランク博士は一九八六年に、二十八日に米衛星が撮影した写真を根拠に「宇宙由来の水」があると提唱したが、当時は証拠不十分として受け入れられなかった。

すい星は通常直径一―十キロで水やメタン、アンモニアなどから成る。研究グループは観測された雪玉もすい星の仲間の微小天体とみている。（共同）

決定的証拠ではない

渡部潤一・国立天文台広報普及室長の話　フランク博士が最初に自説を発表した時、雪玉かどうかをめぐり、研究者の間で大議論になった。今回の観測はその当時のデータに比べ解像度も鋭く説得力があるが、特に一日数千個も飛来するというのは多すぎる。観測は難しいが、慎重にいろいろな証拠を積み上げていくしかないだろう。（共同）

▲1997年6月2日（月）　朝日新聞記事より
Article from the Asahi Shimbun, Monday, June 2, 1997

Water Came from the Space?

The Wonders of Water Become Even Deeper

Evaluating water by taking pictures of water crystals is a new approach that comes from a completely different viewpoint than that of the usual conventional scientific analysis and evaluation methods.
What we learned from these experiments is that we do not know anything about water.
More questions and issues pile up one after another.
Let's start with the questions about the water that exists on earth.
Why does water exist? The origin of water used to be wrapped in mystery.
As the space probe advances, it has already confirmed that water exists on Mars. We are starting to understand that water is not unique to earth but exists all over space.